'This brilliant book penetrates to the heart of the delusions which still obscure the true prospects for our world'.
Peter Jay

'Charles Dumas' and Diana Choyleva's reflections that Europe and China will fall from grace and the US will re-attain it are thought-provoking and convincing. Readers weaned on Dumas' brand of hard-hitting analysis and no-prisoners-taken rigour will not be disappointed.'
David Marsh, author of *The Euro – The Politics of the New Global Currency*

'A forceful global analysis that predicts a wrenching slowdown in China and a troubled decade for Europe but greater resilience for America's economy over the medium term.'
Paul Wallace, *The Economist*

'The tremendous global imbalances in trade and capital flows that have emerged in the past decade - the cause of the crisis affecting the US, Europe, China and the rest of the developing world - are the direct result of policy distortions imposed by a number of governments. Dumas and Choyleva and are among the very few who have consistently understood the source of the imbalances and now explain just why the global adjustment is going to be so difficult, especially for surplus countries.'
Professor Michael Pettis, Guanghua School of Management, Peking University

Praise for *Globalisation Fractures*

'Thank God for Charles Dumas. He displays a true economist's understanding that most things in economics are the opposite of what you would suppose – that for example the global crisis has been as much the work of savings gluttons as of wanton debtors.'
Peter Jay

'Unless we correctly analyse the cause of the current crisis, we will never be able to cure it or prevent a recurrence. Most analysis does not get beneath the symptoms, but Charles Dumas gets to the root problem.'
Peter Lilley

'Charles Dumas has consistently been one of the ablest communicators on the financial crisis – a man with a nose for danger. In characteristically acerbic style he sets out the causes of our distress, seeks out those to blame and maps out the escape routes. Required reading.'
David Marsh

Praise for *The Bill from the China Shop*

'In 2005 Ben Bernanke argued that a global saving glut is causing the huge US current account deficits. Charles Dumas recognised this truth long before him. This splendid book explains how Asia's surpluses are driving US households ever deeper into debt and why this unsustainable process must end in tears.'
Martin Wolf

# THE AMERICAN PHOENIX

## AND WHY CHINA AND EUROPE WILL
## STRUGGLE AFTER THE COMING SLUMP

Charles Dumas and Diana Choyleva

PROFILE BOOKS

First published in Great Britain in 2011 by
Profile Books Ltd
3A Exmouth House
Pine Street
London EC1R 0JH
*www.profilebooks.com*

Typeset in Times by MacGuru Ltd
*info@macguru.org.uk*
Printed and bound in Britain by
Bell & Bain Ltd

A CIP catalogue record for this book is available from the British Library.

ISBN 978 1 84668 564 4
EISBN 978 1 84765 778 7

# Contents

# Figures and tables

# Acknowledgements

Most of the ideas in this book came out of work on the global economy for Lombard Street Research. We owe our colleagues a huge debt for the constant discussion and analysis of ideas, scenarios and forecasts – particularly Brian Reading, whose original work on the flows of funds is a primary tool employed in this book. Brian also has helped keep the emphasis on the damaging role of fixed or managed exchange rates – between China and the US, and within the euro – as a vital mechanism by which China and Germany have pursued 'beggar-my-neighbour' policies for the past decade. Lastly, he helped mightily by editing the prose at key points in this book. When it comes to economic theory, we have adopted a 'pick and choose' approach to the ideas of Keynes, Schumpeter and Friedman, each of whose approaches has great value in thinking about our new crisis, although it must be said that Messrs Keynes and Schumpeter have come out of it better than Friedman – unsurprising historically, as today's problems are much close to the deflation of the 1930s than the inflation of the 1970s.

Our managing director at Lombard Street Research, Peter Allen, aside from his pithy summaries of key issues, has shown his usual insight in helping choose the title for this book: *The*

*American Phoenix* not only catches the longer-run point that the US is the major economy most likely to achieve trend growth over the next five years, but also hints at the 'ashes' that we are forecasting for 2012 – a renewed slump from which countries depending on export-led growth or commodities will scarcely recover for years. The staff of Profile Books have been monuments of good humour and patience, putting up with sometimes dilatory deliveries from the authors, and we are very grateful for that. Lastly, we should thank our respective partners, Pauline Asquith and Dominic Bryant, for putting up with the stress that one inevitably lays off when writing a book.

# Introduction

## The return of imbalances

Global financial imbalances, the fundamental cause of the 2007–09 crisis, have not been reduced in the recovery of 2010–11, merely transformed. The build-up of debt resulting from the new form of imbalances is just as threatening, maybe more so, than that of 2004–07. Then, the excess of saving in the Eurasian savings-glut countries took the world savings rate to the highest level on record in 2006 and 2007. This excessive flow of cash 'crowded out' US savings, which fell to 14% of its GDP in 2007, versus a typical 18%-plus in the 1990s. The flip-side of this was a build-up of overseas US deficits and internal debt, particularly in households, leading to the subprime crisis. Now, the global savings rate, down somewhat by 2009, is back to its 2007 level, and the imbalance has shifted to a grotesque excess of saving by the private sector in all advanced countries, particularly the deficit countries engaged in private-sector debt pay-down ('deleverage'), and nationally in China. The offset to this is huge government deficits throughout the advanced countries and a credit-fuelled investment binge in China. These will ensure financial, but more importantly economic and political, crises and stress throughout the world over the next few years.

The mechanism by which the 2004–07 imbalances arose

was fixed or quasi-fixed exchange rates, specifically China's yuan–dollar peg and Euroland's Economic and Monetary Union (EMU). The great policy discovery of the 1970–2000 period was that free trade and capital movements, with all the benefits they have brought, are only consistent with national autonomy if exchange rates float freely. There has been much loose talk recently about the need for a 'new Bretton Woods'. As Bretton Woods was a fixed exchange-rate system, this is precisely what the world does *not* need. It is through the partial return to fixed exchange rates, with China pegging the yuan to the dollar in 1994 and the arrival of the euro in 1999, that the interactions of what should be autonomous economies have been distorted, resulting in unsustainable imbalances. What the world needs is a return to 'anti-Bretton Woods' – floating rates except where countries linked by fixed rates have genuinely and willingly given up national autonomy. This condition does not and cannot exist between China and the US, and in Europe coordination of policy and behaviour occurs 'more in the breach than the observance': for all the pious talk it is doubtful that Germans want to be like Greeks or Greeks like Germans.

The chief message of this book will be that the US has found a way of making China suffer more for its adoption of a managed yuan–dollar exchange rate than it would have if it had allowed the yuan to float upward. China is discovering the painful reality that the forced combination of China and the US in a common currency zone – imposed unilaterally by China – is deeply destructive. China's unprecedented monetary stimulus that kick-started its economy in 2009 has led more to inflation than to a sustainable boost to growth. Without buoyant US consumer growth, China's muscle-bound focus on low-value exports and over-investment undermines its fast-growth trend. Meanwhile, America's temporary 2011 reflation has exacerbated China's inflationary problems. China's perceived 'win–win' via a deliberately undervalued exchange rate is giving way to real effective appreciation through rapid inflation – for an export-led mercantilist economy a clear 'lose–lose'.

Beijing cannot afford the economic strains and social instability that high inflation would most likely entail. The authorities jumped on the brakes, pushing the economy into a sharp downturn. The Americans, too, will find the shift out of their excessive budget deficits extremely painful, and it is likely to involve a severe slowdown, quite possibly recession, next year. But that adjustment will be made, and it means the end of export-led growth as the chief mechanism of growth and development – in China especially, but also in Europe and in other developing countries that are unable to shift their focus from external competitiveness to strong domestic demand growth.

It is the contention of this book that after 2012 America's vibrant and flexible market economy will enable it to 'rise from the ashes' decisively. The next few years will see China struggle to transform its growth model away from wasteful investment towards consumer spending. The authorities will have to come to terms with much slower growth, but the temptation to go for growth at all cost will be strong, probably resulting in blowing up asset price bubbles, whose eventual bursting will be painful. Chinese average real GDP growth should still outperform that of the US over the next five years, but the US stock market is set to outperform China's. Those investing in China will need a strong stomach for what could be a rollercoaster ride.

The US consumer has been the export market of first resort

for half a century from the 1950s, when its current account typically registered a surplus of 1% of GDP, to five years ago, when
its deficit peaked at 6% of GDP. Now down to a little over 3%
of GDP, this deficit will be replaced by what could well be overseas surplus again in 3–5 years, driven already by, first, major real
effective yuan appreciation as a result of rapid Chinese inflation
and, second, America's incipient budgetary retrenchment. Self-
righteous Asian and European observers have excoriated American
borrowing habits: they should be wary of what they wish for. Easy-
going US import habits have been the foundation of global growth
and emerging market development. America is indeed less powerful than it was. It will be cutting into rates of deficit it can no longer
afford. But for the savings-glut exporters, this will be more damaging than for the US itself – just as was the 2008–09 recession.

A subsidiary message is that Euroland has condemned itself
to a doomed decade. The debt-hobbled economies of the periphery (Ireland and 'Club Med' – Italy, Spain, Greece and Portugal – certainly, and maybe Britain too) cannot expand through
domestic demand growth because of budgetary cutbacks. They
depend on expansion in Germany and the rest of the world. But
the US will be sucking demand out of the rest of the world as it
puts its own finances right. China could see its growth rate halved
to 5% from 10% as its export-led growth model is left sucking
wind. Germany, perhaps even more than China, has stubbornly
refused to accept any modification of its reliance on exports and
will also find itself running on empty, pinning its hopes as it does
on exports to China. Both will find shifting to domestically led
demand as difficult as Japan has over the past 20 years of failed
adjustment. Europe will therefore suffer a continent-wide demand
deficiency at best, and quite possibly depression.

Figure 1    **Gross world saving**
         *% of GDP*

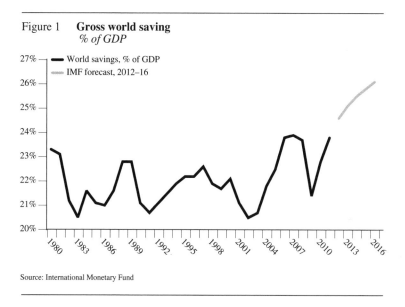

Source: International Monetary Fund

History generally does not repeat itself, but those who do not learn from history may be condemned to something worse than a repeat. The global system of economic governance that survived the so-called Great Recession could well break up when the persistence of damaging global imbalances is revealed by the failure of the current recovery. As the continued imbalances tip the world back into stagnation or recession – forecast for 2012 in this book – a new and very dangerous period of narrow nationalism is the most likely outcome. Globalisation may no longer be 'fractured' – to cite the title of Charles Dumas's book last year – it could be broken and/or reversed.

How have imbalances re-emerged so quickly? The answer is regrettably simple. The original 2004–07 imbalances, and resulting 2007–09 crisis, were ultimately caused, at the level of economic cause and effect, by excess savings in the surplus, savings-glut countries. (Disgraceful bankers' behaviour obviously had an important instrumental role, but in the broad scheme of things their follies and crimes related to the imbalances rather like a drug-running 'mule's' crimes relate to the basic actions of their drug baron bosses.) Consider:

- The world savings rate in 2006–07, when the debt crisis peaked owing to *inadequate* savings in deficit countries, was despite that the highest on record by a large margin at 23.9% of world GDP (Figure 1).
- In the US, the primary debtor country and trigger of the crisis in 2007, growth in the six 'good' years of the cycle after 2001 (the previous, mild recession) averaged a mere 2.6%, compared with a long-run average (*including* recessions) of 3–3¼% consistently achieved over the previous half-century.
- Partly as a result, inflation over those six years averaged a low 2.7% (2.1% excluding food and energy) and had only reached 2.9% at the peak of the cycle in 2007, though the ruinous oil price spike from mid-2007 took the rate temporarily out of the desired 2–3% range in 2008.
- Yet even that low growth and inflation were only achieved with a credit boom that led straight to the crisis – without that credit, growth would have been much lower still.
- In conventional terms it is therefore hard to find major fault with Federal Reserve Board (Fed) policy in 2005–07, although the often idiotic comments of Mr Greenspan were clearly damaging.
- In effect, US policy stabilised the world by offsetting in part the mounting net export surpluses resulting from mercantilist policies in the savings-glut countries – by cutting back its savings rate it limited the rise in global savings that could not find a profitable outlet in the countries doing the excess saving.

- It is tempting to say that without the US dis-saving the record level of world savings in 2007 would have been higher still, but it is more likely that global growth would simply have been much weaker, and with it the level of incomes and saving lower, if not the rate of saving.

- The excess of savings therefore 'crowded out' deficit countries' savings and drove up their debts via continuously low real interest rates, provoking an unjustified asset price boom that appeared to justify the run-up of debt and run-down of savings.

- The persistent low real interest rates are the conclusive *economic* proof that the huge upswing of credit and financial market activity generally was caused by 'supply-push' (excess savings) rather than 'demand-pull' (a spontaneous credit boom) – the latter, had it occurred, would necessarily have dragged up real interest rates in free markets such as government and junk bonds, both of which saw low and falling real yields.

- When the world collapsed into debt-induced recession, the loss of GDP was greater in Japan, China and Germany than in the US or even Britain, clearly demonstrating how the savings-glut countries were even more dependent upon the excessive borrowing of the deficit countries than the latter were themselves.

Alongside the new form of global imbalances – huge private (and Chinese) excess savings and financial surpluses offset by dangerously large government deficits – the world gross savings rate has rebounded from its temporary 2008–09 relapse. Versus 23.9% in 2007 falling to 21.4% in 2009, it is now back to a forecast 23.8% in 2011, as shown in Figure 1, with the International Monetary Fund (IMF) forecasting its steady ascent to a totally unprecedented 26% by 2016. Aside from reviving unsustainable imbalances, this excessive flow of saving is a separate destabilising factor, inducing wasteful investment, most obviously in China.

In Chapters 3 and 4, Diana Choyleva's analysis will demonstrate how this is likely to lead to violent fluctuations in the Chinese economy, with destabilising effects on the rest of the world, as unreasonable growth expectations bump up against the more constrained reality, with enduringly low returns on capital and real interest rates, as too much capital drives down the return on capital. In the real world, the IMF forecast is highly unlikely to come to pass. Much more probable is the forecast of this book that global growth will fall back to virtually nil in 2012, led by Chinese domestic demand that is already slowing sharply through 2011. China may try another massive monetary boost in 2012, but it will lead to overheating and asset prices bubbles even faster than in 2009–10. Over the course of this decade China is set to see much slower growth on average. Much slower growth is also going to beset the emerging countries driven by over-reliance on exports, commodity countries and Europe.

More stupid things are said about saving than most economic subjects – false morality tends to rear its irrelevant head. Without doubt savings are essential to finance investment, and the habit in recent decades of developing countries having much higher savings rates on income than high-income countries therefore makes sense. Developing countries have far more profitable investment outlets for those savings, and doing the savings themselves enhances their autonomy. But the idea that saving is by definition, or invariably, a 'good thing' is economically absurd, and (as it happens) contradicted by the facts. To understand that the excess savings of savings-glut countries can actually cause

Figure 2 **Gross national savings, % of GDP, and real GDP growth**
*1991–2010 averages*

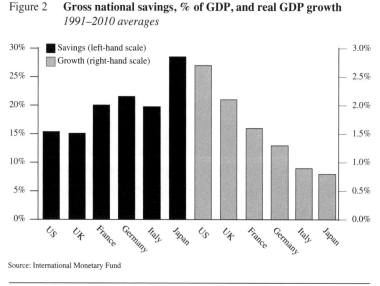

Source: International Monetary Fund

damage on a global scale, the survey shown in Figure 2 helps to illustrate the fatuous waste involved in the high-savings habits of Japan, Germany and Italy. These countries seemingly do not know how to invest profitably at home – nor do they invest effectively abroad.

The macro-economic fall-out of this behaviour is most obviously demonstrated by the German case – Japan is too well known an example to need further emphasis. As detailed in Chapter 6, Germany has crushed its employees' wages and salaries and endured a decade of negligible consumer spending growth to save up money for investment in US subprime mortgages and Greek government bonds. Yet in the process it has aggravated Europe's dangerous imbalances by rendering Club Med countries' labour costs uncompetitive, and taking in a seriously inadequate flow of imports owing to its weak consumer spending. This malevolent combination of 'beggar my neighbour' and 'dog in the manger' is far more immoral than people using their income to enjoy themselves rather than congratulating themselves over their virtue in saving so much.

Why has the recovery since 2009 proved so unbalanced? The answer lies in the refusal of savings-glut countries to take any responsibility for imbalances, blaming the whole sorry episode on excessive borrowing and naughty Anglo-Saxon bankers. A sound recovery would only have occurred if renewed growth in *deficit* countries, most importantly the US, had been accompanied by higher savings rates in those countries to permit reduction of debt. But higher savings rates by definition involve a lessening of domestic demand vis-à-vis domestic product – unless private capital spending were to boom suddenly: an impossible condition, given housing crisis and a depressed economy. But if *domestic* demand vis-à-vis domestic product is to fall back, that product, ie, GDP, can only grow if *external* demand (ie, 'net exports') is increasing (or to be precise, net imports are decreasing). But to reduce net imports in the US and other deficit countries requires a *reduction* of net *exports* in surplus, savings-glut countries. That means their recoveries would have to be led by deliberate, genuine domestic demand expansion. A brief summary of what actually happened, rather than this desirable expansion of surplus countries' domestic demand is:

- Japan would have expanded domestic demand, but for various reasons could not.
- Germany could have, but would not.
- China did for a while, but did so by expanding its already excessive investment even further, rather than generating a genuine

Figure 3    **Advanced Countries financial balances**
            *% of GDP*

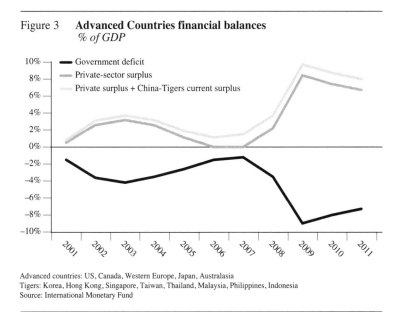

Advanced countries: US, Canada, Western Europe, Japan, Australasia
Tigers: Korea, Hong Kong, Singapore, Taiwan, Thailand, Malaysia, Philippines, Indonesia
Source: International Monetary Fund

consumer-driven recovery, and found that this in combination with insistently maintained undervaluation of its yuan (the yuan–dollar peg) leads to overheating and inflation, forcing renewed domestic restraint.

Because the savings-glut countries failed to expand domestic demand adequately, recovery was achieved by the unhealthy route: government deficit expansion. As the surplus countries were opting out, with the notable exception of China for a while, these fiscal stimuli occurred mostly in the deficit countries. But the aggregate effect is shown in Figure 3. The essence of the recession was a collapse of private spending. To prevent this leading to a self-feeding downward spiral of income and spending, the private sector's ravenous appetite for financial surplus was accommodated by government deficits.

The continued current-account surpluses of China and the Asian Tigers simply added to the needed advanced country government deficits, as Figure 3 illustrates. It was undervaluation of the Chinese yuan that was the chief factor ensuring such continued China/Asian Tiger surpluses, despite China's strong stimulus to domestic demand. In other words, the Chinese stimulus, because it was combined with continued mercantilist insistence on an undervalued yuan, did not stop China and the Asian Tigers from continuing to suck demand out of the rest of the world, notably the advanced countries, in the form of large current-account surpluses. And in the 'real', ie, price-adjusted, terms that affect real growth rates, Figure 4 shows how China's net exports were stronger than even the nominal surplus data suggest – the nominal numbers being held down by a large rise in the cost of its commodity imports.

This massive imbalance, government deficits necessitated by the private sector's need for surplus to pay down its excessive debts and insure against a repeat of 2007–08's peril, is the chief source of jeopardy to the world economy – though some European countries, notably Ireland, Portugal and Spain, and also Britain, remain at risk from excessive private sector debts (see Chapters 5 and 7 and the Appendix). The smooth further global recovery forecast by most official institutions and governments depends on the assumption that the private sector surpluses will shrink spontaneously and rapidly in 2011–13 as debts are paid down and the desire for precautionary surpluses is satiated. The IMF's forecast, for example, has the private surplus of the advanced countries halving from 7½% of GDP to 3¾% between 2010 and 2013, even though only a minimal part of this shift is projected for 2011, the first of the three years. It is a major theme of this book that this is unlikely to be the case – particularly and crucially in the US. In the event, while US private surpluses are likely to stay high, strong fiscal tightening next year could slow its economy sharply, and transmit deflation to the rest of the world.

Chapter 1 therefore shows how the failure of surplus, savings-glut countries to assume responsible global leadership in supporting the recovery – together with an aggressive 'blame game' to attempt to pin responsibility for the world's problems solely on borrowers – has given way to a re-assertion of tradition in the form of American leadership. And it will remain American leadership with American interests to the fore, in response to the ruthlessly self-interested persistence of the Chinese leadership in pursuing its mercantilist cheap-yuan policy. Washington has turned the tables on Beijing by using monetary and fiscal reflation to add a huge dose of cost–push inflation to China's major demand–pull domestic overheating that is the natural, indeed inevitable result of a seriously undervalued currency. But US fiscal policy, involving a major deflation of demand next year, will impose great pain on both its own citizens and the world at large, so the near future contains economic and political upheavals with unfathomable consequences.

Ultimately, the global focus of policy on the removal of deficits means most importantly hefty retrenchment of US fiscal deficits. In a world of already record-high savings, such cuts in spending – either by governments or through tax increases on households – naturally imply recession. US deficit cuts will quickly lead to the destruction of the primary condition for the past success of the export-led growth model: large US net imports. The rest of the book will be devoted to the likely consequences: world recession next year as a result of strong US fiscal tightening and Chinese inflation, followed by re-emergence of the US as the world's most successful economy, and sustained failure of China, Germany and probably Japan to achieve satisfactory growth.

Alongside the come-uppance of the savings-glut countries, the dangerous debt burdens of various countries will be analysed. Some of them are now concentrated in government debt and deficits – the obvious cases being Greece, Japan and maybe Italy. But the danger for others still lurks largely in the private sector – this group including Ireland, Portugal, Spain, and Britain. All of these countries have worse debt problems than the much discussed US case. One natural result of the forecast halving of Chinese growth, only moderate recovery in America and a probable decade of nil growth in Europe is an end to the 12-year run-up of oil and metal prices (excluding gold, which is money not a commodity). But the dim prospects for the Asian emerging markets that have focused too intensely on export-led growth overlap with likely downswings in commodity countries to leave only a modest range of countries whose medium-term prospects look rosy. These issues, and a list of reforms and actions needed to avert or mitigate the damage forecast here, will be summarised in the concluding chapter.

# I

# America shakes China loose

After the 2007–09 crisis, the US needed devaluation and tighter domestic policy to sustain recovery and growth while cutting excessive debts built up in the pre-crisis 'gilded age'. Likewise, other deficit nations, notably Britain, Ireland, and Club Med. But that could only happen if surplus countries readily increased their domestic demand, which they did not – frustrated in China's case by the clear contradiction between stimulating domestic demand and maintaining a deliberately undervalued exchange rate. Instead of following such a healthy path, the recovery that we have had so far has depended largely on deficit countries' willingness to run large government deficits. This effectively transfers debt from private to public hands, rather than reducing it through rising national savings rates. Sustaining these government deficits over the medium term would lead to unacceptably high government debt. As and when countries take steps to cut budget deficits, growth is likely to be cut – to sub-par with luck, recession more probably.

The healthy path, with deficit countries' recoveries led by net exports, depended on policy changes by their opposite numbers, the surplus countries with savings gluts – China, Japan, the Asian Tigers, Germany and the north-central European countries round

Figure 4    **Real net exports**
*4-quarter moving averages, 2005 constant prices*

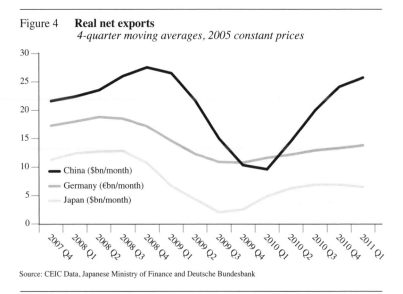

Source: CEIC Data, Japanese Ministry of Finance and Deutsche Bundesbank

Germany (Benelux, Nordics, Switzerland and Austria). For deficit countries to grow by net exports, or rather by reduced net imports, surplus countries must *reduce* their net exports: the total of the world's trade surpluses and deficits is necessarily zero. Lesser net exports in savings-glut, surplus countries almost certainly required and requires higher real exchange rates, a logic that only Japan has accepted. Yet expansion based on domestic demand is something Japan would do, but cannot (though the recent disasters have, with unpleasant irony, increased the chances of a good outcome); Germany could do it, but will not; and China did it for a while in spring, 2009, but could not sustain the downward trend of net export volume because of its undervalued currency, lapsing into overheating and inflation. Figure 4 shows how the second, third and fourth largest economies in the world have continued to increase their net exports, thwarting healthy recovery in the

Figure 5    **Financial balances in the US economy**
             *% of GDP*

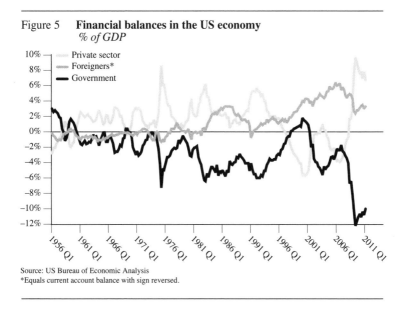

Source: US Bureau of Economic Analysis
*Equals current account balance with sign reversed.

US, Britain, Club Med and other deficit countries – and, soon, themselves.

While this is a fair description of post-crisis global recovery to date, by a peculiar inversion of policy – domestic stimulus to provoke effective devaluation, rather than devaluation with domestic tightening – the US seems to have loosened the grip that China, with its policy of clamping its yuan onto the dollar, has exerted on US policy autonomy. As a result, America is at the same time imposing on China a double measure of the natural effect of its policy – inflation – and giving itself the possibility of reasonable medium-term growth. The real exchange rate of the dollar is being lowered by the back-door, Chinese inflation. But the price of this year's US stimulus is that next year could see a severe US relapse, as policy returns to the necessary cuts in domestic consumption, via higher taxes and reduced government spending.

It is one of many ironies in the current crisis that the US has had to do the opposite of what any outside observer – either a man from Mars or, indeed, the IMF – would recommend: 'devalue and tighten your belt'. Figure 5 leads immediately to that conclusion. In effect though, because of the yuan–dollar peg, the US has been forced to devalue by 'loosening its belt'. But the need for lesser US domestic deficits and debt, ie, higher US savings, remains in place. So now, with devaluation achieved, via Chinese real appreciation disguised as inflation, the US has to tighten its belt – especially as it will suffer significant imported inflation from Chinese imports, imported inflation being invariably part of the price of devaluation. It is this dynamic that will be analysed in this and the next chapter.

The world has two major sources of imbalances, split roughly 60:40. The major, global imbalance is between the US and China, with its Japanese and Asian Tiger camp followers. Within Europe, the somewhat smaller, but proportionately equal, maybe greater, imbalance is between the north-central group of countries round (and led by) Germany and Club Med. Both these imbalances were rooted in national habits, attitudes and polices before 2007, but both are also the direct result of fixed or semi-fixed exchange rates: the Chinese yuan's peg to the dollar and the euro system.

The lack of freely floating exchange rates between countries with strongly different behaviour patterns and policies was a major source of the build-up of imbalances in the run-up to the 2007–08 crisis, as well as the lack of healthy adjustment and recovery since. Some similarities with the 1971 collapse of the Bretton Woods system of fixed exchange rate were evident. Both Chinese exchange-rate policy and the rashly broad membership of the euro represent denial of the basic point, established over three decades from 1971, that the combination of free trade and capital movements with national economic policy autonomy is only possible with floating exchange rates. This is true in general, but illustrated particularly unpleasantly when the countries yoked together in a common currency (or currency zone such as China/America, 'Chimerica') are massively different in character: eg, level of income, tendency to inflation, growth potential, willingness to accept migration, even language.

To illustrate the point by its opposite, the Dutch guilder was tied to the deutschmark (DM) for decades before the exchange rate mechanism (ERM), euro, etc, were conceived of, reflecting the similarity and compatibility of the two economies, and Holland's relatively small size. The Dutch accepted that their monetary policy autonomy was negligible – likewise, obviously, exchange rate policy – and the Dutch Central Bank was effectively a branch office of the Bundesbank. This turned out to matter rather a lot when North Sea gas was discovered – so much so that the problems of an economy with a sudden discovery of large, valuable mineral wealth has ever since been known as the 'Dutch disease'. Unlike sudden such discoveries, the unsuitability of combining China with America in a single currency zone, or Club Med with Germany, were blatantly obvious from the start and simply ignored by ignorant and arrogant politicians.

Or was it? Were they, rather, trying to exercise low cunning? In the Chimerica case, which is a policy solely imposed by Beijing against continued US objections, China's undervalued exchange rate arose largely by accident – the yuan was fixed in 1994 as a stabilisation measure after major devaluation to deal with inflation that had reached 30% the year before. But the explosive growth of China's manufacturing capacity, and its large pool of rural-unemployed cheap labour, ensured that within ten years China's exports were expanding far faster than its rapid, 10% annual GDP advance, or even than its even more rapidly mounting imports. The mobilisation of this cheap labour led to falling prices of Chinese exports at an average rate of 1½% a year in 1995–2004, while other countries had positive inflation. Where the low cunning comes in is that preserving the accidentally acquired undervaluation of the yuan seemed like a free ride – the much sought-after 'win–win' of economic policy. This natural mercantilist desire for an easy ride through undervalued currency was also part of the calculation of many Germans as the euro was conceived. Germany was overvalued in the 1990s, after reunification. It did not take profound insight to see that in a currency union with Mediterranean countries their inflation would exceed Germany's, making the latter more cost-competitive.

If the mercantilists were right that an undervalued currency is a 'win–win', then competitive devaluation would be a permanent bane. But of course they are not, as the Bundesbank understood in the pre-euro days of the rising DM. Germany gained hugely in the old days from letting its real exchange rate rise (ie, the trade-weighted rate adjusted for relative inflation). It kept inflation low, and spurred business to productivity gains that were then reflected in a higher standard of living for ordinary Germans. Even in the difficult and destabilised 1990s after reunification, German growth of both output and real consumption was greater than over the period since the euro started in 1999. In fact, over the latest full economic cycle, as German cost competitiveness has been enhanced, real German consumer spending has hardly risen at all, and its overall economy, including the highly competitive exports, was slower than Japan's. Neither will Germany grow fast over the next decade, on current policies and behaviour patterns, as we shall demonstrate in Chapters 5 and 6. So much for the 'win–win' of undervaluation.

An economy that has gained recently from overvalued currency is Britain's. Scarred by the humiliation of expulsion from the euro's predecessor, the ERM, in 1992, floating rates were accepted with relief. The real exchange rate of the pound rose in 1996–97 to some 20% over its 'right rate' or long-term equilibrium value, remaining there for the ten years to 2007. This was crucial, driven partly by interest rates kept above euro rates by the intensity of the housing and consumption boom. Overvaluation added to the restraint arising from those higher interest rates that were intended to curb overheating in the economy and capital markets, notably housing. The excessive boom that in any case seriously overshot sustainable growth rates would have been far more violent without the higher-than-euro interest rates and overvalued pound. Overvalued sterling served Britain well – as the contrast with Ireland's extravagant carnival within, and exacerbated by, the euro illustrates only too painfully.

It is a crucial part of the argument of this book to demonstrate that the undervaluation of China and Germany achieved by fixed exchange rates will prove extremely costly to them over the next several years, in contrast to their relatively benign experience since the trough of the recession in early 2009. Just as the US needs the devaluation that Beijing policy constrains, China and Germany need the adjustment to higher consumption and less net exports and investment that is the normal accompaniment to a higher real exchange rate.

It is valuable to distinguish between the process by which an exchange rate imbalance develops and the resulting period of adjustment. The undervaluation of China and Germany arose in different ways, and culminated in the imbalances we have today. That was pre-crisis, in the past. Now, post-crisis, the imbalance is there for everybody to see. The question becomes what happens next – on the assumption of no major exchange rate adjustment, either yuan/dollar or intra-euro. The initial stage of the answer is clear. Either the overvalued part of the fixed-currency zone gets deflation, or the undervalued part gets inflation, or a bit of both. As a result, the real exchange rates start to adjust back towards the right rates.

By the summer of 2010, after a year of recovery, it seemed likely that a US lapse into deflation would be part of the resolution of the Chimerica imbalance, though Chinese inflation was also clearly a mounting problem. The US seemed condemned to inadequate growth over several years, as the inability to achieve devaluation meant that getting the budget deficit, over 10% of GDP, under control as well as achieving the needed higher personal savings rate must lead to an enduring restriction of demand, output and incomes. The cuts in net imports over time would come not from the desirable source – devaluation and tight policy, diverting output to net exports – but from simple deflation of demand and, eventually, prices.

Between August and December, 2010, this outlook was changed dramatically in both directions – and the inflationary cost of undervaluation and excessive reliance on exports was brought home to China and Germany. As it happens, US motivation in both monetary and fiscal policy changes appears to have been largely parochial and domestic, yet their chief benefits may prove to be their global effects. Most importantly, the adoption of a renewed bout of quantitative easing of the money supply in autumn 2010 (QE2, QE1 being the policy over the winter and spring of 2008–09) seems likely to transform global imbalances. The bout of fiscal ease then adopted in December, 2010, linked to the two-year extension of President Bush junior's 2003 tax cuts, has created a temporary boom–bust scenario for the domestic US economy that is dominating 2011–12. The 2011 boom phase has aggravated China's inflation problem, and helped create one for Germany. The next phase, bust in 2012, will penalise their export dependence. This penalty for export dependence seems likely to endure for several years at least. When German Finance Minister Schäuble described US QE2 as 'clueless' he may have been looking in the mirror.

The immediate effects of US Fed Chairman Bernanke 'trailing' his intention of adopting QE2 in late-August 2010 was a jump of 20–25% in food commodity prices, crude oil, and the stock market. The euro and yen went up sharply, and the dollar had a trade-weighted fall of 4–5% even though China's yuan went down with it. The result, for China, was disturbing. Inflation had already replaced deflation before QE2 came along. Its inflation rate, minus 1.9% in the year to summer 2009, had swung round by 5½ percentage points to rise 3½% in the year to August, 2010, reflecting the economy's overheating as domestic stimulus was combined with major export recovery. Food prices were up 7½% already. By three months later, food price inflation was well into double figures and overall consumer prices up 5%-plus, against a government target of 3% that was hastily revised to 4%.

Food is one seventh (14%) of the US consumer price index (CPI), and much of the total value comprises food processing and retailing rather than raw commodity content. In China it is one third (33%) and with much greater pure commodity-price content. US QE2 altered the balance in the US-deflation/Chinese-inflation effect of the currency imbalance. China may have artificially clamped its yuan onto the dollar to create Chimerica, but the US controls the currency – and was thus in a position to make it Chinese inflation, more than US deflation, that rectifies the imbalance over time. The yuan's link to the dollar was suddenly no longer a free ride. The initiative that had appeared to lie entirely in Beijing has turned out not to be so one-sided – as one would expect: it was always a mistake to expect America to remain passive once the downside of global imbalances became evident. China's overheating already represented a serious demand/pull inflation problem. US QE2 gave China's inflation a good cost–push kick upwards.

It is a fundamental point of the run-up to the 2007–08 crisis that America was passive, while the savings-glut countries actively pursued export-led expansion. The result of the excess of global savings (which reached an all-time high in 2006–07 as a percent of world output) was that deficit countries, led by the US, were offered cheap money – to buy cheap goods, whose prices were being held down or even reduced by globalisation and the mobilisation of low-cost labour in emerging economies. Unwisely sure of the automatic self-stabilising capacity of the world and domestic economy, the US complacently drifted along, enjoying a surge of asset price gains and debt-financed consumption. A key point of the post-crisis situation is that this US *laissez-faire* passivity has gone for good.

Already by late-autumn 2010 the boost to stock markets from the trailing and implementation (from early November) of QE2 had contributed to a wealth effect that took the US personal savings rate down by nearly 1%, fuelling a burst of high-end consumer spending. Then in early December 2010 President Obama negotiated major tax cuts in exchange for giving the Republicans, newly triumphant after November Congressional election victories, the two-year extension of the entirety of President Bush junior's 2003 tax cuts that were then due to expire (a goal they were set on). One of these tax cuts was a simple one-year reduction of social security contributions to be reversed in January 2012. The second was a measure that is provoking a late-2011 surge of business spending, but whose reversal in 2012 is likely to cause a slump in activity next year. This was the granting of 100% first-year depreciation for 2011 only – ie, treating fixed investment as a current expense.

The full story of how this ability to deduct the full cost of new equipment in its year of purchase, rather than gradually over its working life, is told in Chapter 2. Suffice it to say here that a portion of what would have been 2012 capital spending is being brought forward into 2011 to enjoy the benefit of this temporary tax break. As a result, output is booming in late 2011. But this spending will not merely cease in early 2012: in addition, the spending then will be cut further because some of the equipment that would normally have been bought then will already have been installed in 2011 to get the tax break. This policy is thus a 'doomsday' machine for boom–bust, with the bust coming, uncomfortably for Mr Obama, some nine months ahead of the Presidential election. While growth in late-2011 is likely to be strong, a recession is entirely possible in 2012 before the economy returns to an even keel.

The US boom–bust arising from expensing business investment will be aggravated by at least four other factors – self-reinforcing in the case of interaction with China. Strong US growth adds to Chinese overheating and inflation, necessitating more strenuous restrictive policies to quell price and wage excesses. With the Chinese leadership changeover from Messrs Hu and Wen also due in November, 2012, and the desire to hand over a 'clean slate', a Chinese domestic demand downswing is likely in parallel with, if not before, the US during the winter of 2011/12. This will slow world trade and cut into US exports.

The second point is that America's restoration in 2012 of the pre-2011 rate of social security contributions will amount to a tax increase (of ¾% of GDP). Third, the level of government spending is being cut, with strenuous political battles over federal spending levels – though all seem to agree on the need for cuts. Meanwhile, state and local spending is subject to enforced reduction owing to excessive debts and deficits. The shift in US fiscal policy, higher taxes and lower spending, is estimated at 2½% of GDP in just one year, 2012 versus 2011 – a huge restrictive move in the world's largest economy. Lastly, the mid-2011 build-up of business investment is using up a significant part of what was until early-2011 a surplus of cash flow that had been pouring liquidity into financial markets. And this reduction of liquidity has roughly coincided with the removal of the Fed's QE2 in mid-2011. This squeeze on liquidity already seems to be topping out the two-year stock-market recovery from March 2009 until recently.

This strongly fluctuating US demand pattern means that 2011 is, or should be, a banner year for the export-led, savings-glut economies. For China, however, this adds extra inflationary demand to an economy already overheated and plagued by the cost–push of food, energy and metal price inflation arising from QE2. The short-term Chinese situation and outlook is described in Chapter 4, but the key point is that China's undervaluation means that an on-trend rate of advance in the world economy is likely to cause acceleration of inflation in China. China will no doubt take the steps to stop inflation getting out of control. But these will both require aggressive and unpopular restraint of demand and jeopardy for export-industry profits, and will almost certainly leave Chinese inflation in any case significantly higher than the US.

After a burst of strong relative Chinese-over-US inflation in 2010–12, relative costs could continue to rise. But already the US is achieving a real effective devaluation vis-à-vis China – or China a real effective appreciation vis-à-vis the US – through the 'back-door' of Chinese inflation. In early 2011, China's export prices were up 10% from the year before. Its industrial profit margins were down, meaning unit labour costs were rising faster, more than 10%. Yet in the US unit labour costs in business have been static to falling for more than two years. This 10% relative shift in home-currency unit labour costs, combined with some 5% Beijing-controlled appreciation of the yuan, means China's bilateral relative unit labour costs have been appreciating at up to a 15% annual rate for more than a year. This does not need to go on much longer to permit the US the real trade-weighted devaluation it needs. Notably, also, this inflation is much more noxious for China's economy and key segments of the population than the simple acceptance of currency appreciation that has been so furiously rejected. So China, with its deliberate undervaluation of the yuan, has 'shot itself in the foot'.

There are two crucial conclusions from this story so far. First, when a price has ended a long swing away from equilibrium, its return to, and through, equilibrium is almost inexorable. Thus the Chinese undervaluation and US overvaluation are virtually bound to unwind, and Beijing's attempts to prevent or retard the increase in the relative value of Chinese incomes vis-à-vis American is bound to fail. Indeed, in any welfare-orientated view of China's economy, it is desirable that it should fail. (The parallel logic for Germany and its euro 'partners' will be laid out later, in Chapters 5 and 6.) Second, the US, now it has 'woken up', has policy tools at its disposal for reducing global imbalances, and enforcing the post-Bretton-Woods system: free trade, and capital movements with floating exchange rates to permit national autonomy in monetary policy. The regressive yearning for fixed rates is likely to prove damaging to its perpetrators, not beneficial as they hope.

The medium-term, 3–5 year, drivers of the US economy are interactive demographic and financial forces. The population chart 'bulges' with the baby-boomers, people born from 1946 to 1964 (in the US and Britain, later elsewhere). The detailed argument is in Chapter 2, but the key point is that the baby-boomers have neither the inclination (in many cases) nor the savings (in most cases) to retire. As a result, they will hang onto their jobs, making it hard for younger people and potentially holding up unemployment for several years. This implies downward pressure on wages and salaries, and possibly continuation of the recent upward trend in profits as a share of GDP. Also, as the still-working baby-boomers will be rescuing their finances, the savings rate could go up. So consumer spending could fall as a share of GDP. Meanwhile a government deficit of over 10% of GDP undoubtedly means that government spending will see its share heavily cut. As business investment depends partly on the perception of future sales, it too could be relatively restrained. So the only element of demand left, net exports, will necessarily increase. (The expression 'increasing net exports' in a US context means, of course, falling net imports.) Owing to the likely achievement of a lower real US exchange rate, this should take the form of export growth and import substitution, but only after the slump-induced import crash that we expect for 2012.

Financial flows shown in Figure 5 (p. 17 above) point to the same conclusion. The budget deficit is 10% of GDP. Two (of the three) counterparts are nearly 2% of GDP for the surplus of household savings over housing investment and 5% of GDP for the surplus of business savings over non-residential investment. Together these give a private sector surplus of 7%. The difference with the 10% budget deficit is accounted for by (slightly over) 3% of GDP for the current account deficit, or 'foreigners' surplus' (vis-à-vis the US).

How are these elements likely to develop in future? We have seen that business margins are likely to remain strong after a 2012 slump-induced dip, while business investment is unlikely to boom after 2011. So the business surplus could remain high, though it will have come down somewhat in 2012. The household savings rate should be increasing as the baby-boomers work on, and a major housing revival is far off, so the household surplus of 2% of GDP could rise. This means the private sector surplus of 7% may come down a little, but probably not much. But the government deficit will have to come down to a maximum of 4% of GDP if the public sector *debt* ratio to GDP is to be stopped from rising in a few years' time, by which time it will have reached an alarming 100%. If the private surplus is to be not much less than 7% and the budget deficit 4% or less, the current account will be in surplus in 3–5 years' time. This may seem an extreme scenario, but on any reckoning the US current-account deficit, which was on an upward trend for 50 years until its peak at around 6% of

GDP in 2005–06, is likely to be minimal by the middle of the coming decade.

This is the challenge to the export-led economies. For 50 years from the 1950s, Daddy America pump-primed their economies with his imports, permitting their export-led advances – first Germany, then Japan, Korea, the Asian Tigers and, most recently, China. But Daddy can no longer afford it – he will no longer be bank-rolling other countries' easy, export-led growth. The US consumer will no longer be the market of first resort. There is very little sign that the savings-glut countries are in any way aware, let alone prepared, for this new world order – or disorder. The remainder of this book will detail the ways in which they seem unequal to the challenge. As the commodity boom and commodity countries are also dependent for their recent wealth on the export-led economies, notably China, it follows that the upward cycle since 1999 in commodity prices is probably close to an end. Part of the improvement in the US trade balance could arise from less costly imports, improving real US incomes, rather than the whole of it reflecting trade volumes. The developing economies that are less threatened by this medium-term outlook are those that base their economic expansion primarily on domestic demand – India, much of Latin America, Turkey and Indonesia, etc. And the day when China's GDP overtakes that of the US is probably far more distant than is widely supposed.

# 2

# American boom–bust,
# then healthy growth

Our medium-term (3–5-year) forecast of US growth, probably averaging close to its 2½% trend, opens with a probable boom–bust in 2011–12. A fundamental point is that 2011's good prospects depend on late-2010's QE2-related relapse of US personal saving being reinforced by an additional government fiscal stimulus enacted last December. Both these changes undo part of the post-crisis upward adjustment of US saving (in any case far from complete) that will nevertheless have to be resumed in due course. However, the fiscal stimulus that is widening the deficit applies to 2011 only. The measures reverse automatically in January 2012. Meanwhile the new Republican majority in the House of Representatives has the Administration and the Senate's Democrat majority on the back foot over federal spending, which in any scenario is going to be cut significantly. Further budgetary tightening within the overall public sector is already occurring through the compression of state and local spending, in response to both balanced budget laws and difficulties raising debt in the financial markets. The total deflationary shift in public-sector policies – the so-called 'structural', cyclically corrected fiscal balance – is estimated by the IMF to be 2½% of GDP in just one year, between 2011 and 2012: a massively restrictive package by any standards.

In 2012, this government fiscal tightening and households' probable reversion to increased saving is likely to be reinforced by a sharp drop in business spending. This business-spending up–down reflects a much sharper specific point than simply the knock-on effects of the general economy. A first-year depreciation allowance of the full 100% of capital spending on assets with 20 years' operating life or less has been introduced for 2011 only (after which it returns to 50–60% first-year) creating a powerful incentive to bring business capital spending forward from 2012 into 2011. This intensifies the likely upswing in GDP at end-2011, and suggests an even stronger fallback of such spending in 2012, as demand shifts downward doubly, from being boosted by the brought-forward spending to being reduced by its absence.

## 2011/12 boom–bust: the battle of the budget

The violent up–down effects of 100% depreciation are prospectively similar to, but larger than, the effects of 'cash for clunkers' (in which people were encouraged by a cash payment to bring forward replacement of decrepit old cars). But the general stance of fiscal policy fosters strength in 2011 and threatens weakness in 2012. This affects consumer spending, government spending and exports, as well as capital expenditure (cap-ex). For consumer spending, we first saw a sharp boost from the drop in the personal savings rate from a peak (excluding tax-rebate months) of 6.3% in June 2010. This is widely ascribed to a wealth effect arising from the 25–30% stock market rally after Mr Bernanke's

Jackson Hole speech 'trailing' QE2, though depressed housing pointed the other way. A point in favour of this view is that the late-2010 consumer growth was concentrated in high-end goods and services, plausibly connecting it to stock market strength. It outweighed the cut in real consumer incomes from another QE2 consequence, higher food and energy prices.

Now, monthly during 2011, we have seen a temporary cut in employees' social security deductions equivalent to nearly 1% of total personal disposable income. Thus, consumer income is boosted in 2011(but then cut back in early 2012, when the social security charges return to their normal rate). Middle-Eastern political instability qualifies this in that it sharply boosted oil prices in spring 2011, with gasoline prices boosted a seasonally adjusted 15% in the three months after the Libyan crisis started to affect the market in mid-February. As gasoline alone accounts for nearly 5% of the US cost of living, this offset much of the benefit of the social security tax reduction in spring 2011. But as the danger of major political upheaval spreading to the (much more important) oil producers in the Gulf has faded, oil prices have fallen back, thus reviving the growth of real consumer incomes in the second half of 2011. This inhibition of second-quarter demand, with its revival in the summer quarter, is reinforced by the effects of Japan's triple disasters in March (earthquake, tsunami and nuclear melt-down). These led to severe global shortages of key components in the automobile and high-tech industries that curtailed output in the spring. But Japanese (and other) resourcefulness led to the lost output being made up in the summer.

Reinforcing the positive 2011 outlook, exports have responded to the renewed boom in world trade since autumn 2010. China's overheating is ensuring increasingly restrictive policies, but the momentum of its past growth has kept world trade growth strong, with buoyancy in the emerging markets and commodity countries. US exports have grown faster than GDP as a result.

It is not possible to estimate with any precision the amount of business spending that will be brought forward into 2011 by 100% year-1 write-offs. In principle, if a firm was going to buy a truck in February 2012, say, or April, it would probably be well advised to buy it in November 2011 instead, to get the full cost deductible at the 35% corporate tax rate in 2011. The same applies to computers, other high-tech equipment and software. The key question is the balance between the interest-rate cost of buying the equipment earlier than it is needed, versus the value of receiving a 100% tax deduction in 2011 rather than a flow of tax deductions spread over the life of the asset (using the normal rules of the Internal Revenue Service (IRS), including the fact that 2012 cap-ex will be permitted to use a 50–60% first-year depreciation deduction before amortising the remaining 40–50% over subsequent years in the normal fashion).

Without detailing the calculations here, the conclusions suggest a large effect is possible. It is cost-effective to bring spending forward by about half a year in the case of short-life assets that normally depreciate over five years; and by roughly a full year for longer-life assets. The five-year group covers more than 4% of GDP in equipment and software spending, the over-five-year group less than 4%. Of this total for capital spending on equipment and software (8% of GDP) it is therefore theoretically economic for 5–6% of 2012 GDP to be brought forward into 2011 on top of the normal flow of such spending that would anyhow occur. Of course, these calculations assume that buying 2012 and subsequent years' kit in 2011 creates no price-inflation, delivery, quality or cash-flow problems. Importantly, it also ignores sheer inertia. It is highly unlikely that such a large pull-forward of 2012 spending will actually occur, so 'guesstimates' have to be made for illustrative purposes. The force of the 100% write-off effect can be gauged by simply assuming only 1% of 2012 GDP (rather than 5–6%) is brought forward into 2011, with three quarters of it in the last quarter of the year, and one quarter of it in the summer quarter (2011 Q3).

The first point to make is that 1% of 2012 GDP relates to full-year GDP: 1% of full-year GDP is 4% of quarterly GDP. So the three quarters of the effect occurring in 2011's fourth quarter will swell its GDP by 3% from what it would otherwise have been. But as growth during 2011 could be at a 2½–3% rate, this cap-ex effect means fourth-quarter GDP would be up 5½–6% from 2010's fourth quarter. (The rate of growth from quarter to quarter, calculated on the American convention of raising quarterly growth rates to annual equivalents, would be much higher still, possibly in double figures as a percentage.) As the 100% write-off effect is assumed to be significant in the third quarter of 2011 and then large in the fourth, it could have the semblance of a boom.

Sadly, even more than with most booms, the 'bust' in this scenario follows immediately and drastically. In the first quarter of 2012, GDP will be reduced not just by the loss of the 3% 'premium' in the previous quarter. It will also be even further down because a significant portion of the capital spending brought forward into 2011 would ordinarily have occurred in the first quarter of 2012. As the total amount taken into 2011 was 4% of *quarterly* GDP, if even half of that came out of the first quarter of 2012 the loss would be 2%, on top of the 3% loss of the 'premium'. So GDP could fall by amounts approaching 5% in early 2012 – and nearly four times that when expressed in the American fashion as an annual rate. By the end of 2012, this 'loss-effect' should have largely gone away, and the underlying growth of GDP could remain 2½–3% from the end of 2011. But the loss of 2011's fourth-quarter 'premium' could still leave end-2012 GDP at or below the end-2011 level. In effect, what could look like a recession may prove hard to avoid, given the simultaneous restrictive effect of the social-security tax increase scheduled for January 2012, strong potential cuts in public spending, and a world trade slowdown as China comes to grips with its inflation problem.

While the analysis of this depreciation-induced up–down in business cap-ex has been based on the conjecture that 1% of GDP will be shifted from 2012 into 2011, the scale of this shift could be larger or smaller. What seems clear is that the effects of this tax policy will create a large fluctuation of the type described here, even if the size of it is inevitably speculative. Countries have allowed 100% depreciation before, but its availability for such a short period and with such a clear cut-off date set in advance, in a financially sophisticated business environment, makes this unprecedented. All one can say with confidence is that as an influence on short-term growth rates it is likely to be major, both upward and downward, if unquantifiable in advance. And it reinforces other aspects of fiscal policy, loose in 2011, much tighter in 2012, including likely cuts in government spending.

The US federal budget year starts in October, so from then at the latest spending cuts could start, promised aggressively by Tea Party members, less assertively by mainstream Republicans (whose track record shows easy tolerance of budget deficits). This

Figure 6    **US government receipts and outlays**
            *% of GDP*

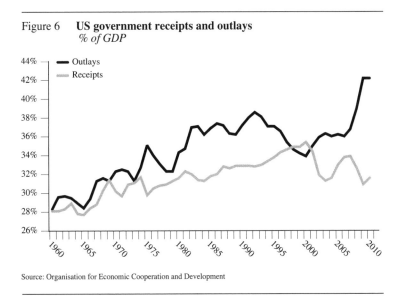

Source: Organisation for Economic Cooperation and Development

suggests a major and apparently endless political battle. Clearly, Republicans will wish to avoid their fate in similar circumstances under Newt Gingrich's leadership in 1995: he shut down the government by refusing to approve budget spending, enabling President Clinton to be re-elected easily in 1996. But Democrats as well as Republicans have committed themselves to cuts in spending. It must be assumed that real federal spending will be cut in 2012, contributing to the likely sharp economic slowdown.

Nor is it political extremism to demand a reduced share of public spending in US GDP. Figure 6 shows that the imbalance of US budgeting in recent years has largely taken the form of a much greater GDP share of government spending, rather than a lesser share of taxes. Total government spending in 2010 was nearly 4% of GDP higher than any previous year (except 2009) and 6% of GDP higher than the prevailing level before the 2007–09 crisis.

A vast majority of Americans wish to see government deficits brought within bounds, and debt ratios to income stabilised (at least, preferably reduced), over a medium-term timeframe. In the event, the cuts may have already started. Early 2011 GDP data showed real government spending down, with state and local predictably lower, but also major cuts in defence spending. This is likely to be the start of a trend, rather than a one-off.

The force of this fiscal squeeze should not be underestimated. For example, the IMF's estimate of the structural budget deficit of all sectors of the US government – state and local, as well as federal – is that it will shrink from 8.1% of GDP in 2011 to 5.7% in 2012, a major 2½ percentage-point reduction. Only an economy with very strong upward momentum could withstand such a violent fiscal squeeze – and the whole point of the 100% year-1 write-off analysis is that it will create the opposite of upward momentum: a strong downdraught.

## Medium-term deleverage to resume

Prior to the fiscal stimulus tacked onto the early-December extension of Bush tax cuts, US growth at a 2% rate or maybe less seemed likely for the 3–5-year medium term. Achievement of real effective devaluation, as described in Chapter 1, raises the chances of the outcome being closer to the trend rate of 2½%. The strong 2011–12 cyclical boom–bust prospect described in this review so far leaves that view little changed over the average of the two years to the end of 2012. The faster growth projected for 2011 should generate some self-sustaining momentum, but the major scale of the headwinds likely between mid-2011 and mid-2012 could slow growth to a crawl, if not actual recession, by mid- to late-2012. The scale of the up–down effect on demand of 100% first-year depreciation is open to serious doubts in either direction. But the overall impact of it is likely to be small in the medium term, beyond 2012.

The four medium-term forces that could govern the next 3–5 years are:

1. Achievement of lower relative US labour costs via the 'back-door' of Chinese inflation.
2. Demographics, faster labour force growth as baby-boomers stay at work, reflecting …
3. Continued need for higher US personal savings, to finish the needed cuts in household debt and rebuild assets.
4. Budget balancing, to slow or stop the escalation of government debt.

## China's inflation – real effective dollar depreciation

Relative cost competitiveness of countries is a blend of currency movements and the change in labour costs of a country relative to those of its trading partners. The primary need of the US is to generate growth by net exports, permitting the national savings rate to rise without depressing demand, growth and employment. The policy to achieve this would be devaluation, enabling growth to continue while excessive deficits are reduced. This policy was thwarted by America's main exchange rate being set in Beijing. The flip-side of China's deliberate undervaluation by pegging its yuan to the dollar is that the US dollar is overvalued. By mid-2010 this appeared to condemn the US either to breaching the global free trade rules, or accepting sub-par growth and excessive government deficits for several years.

Most other countries, confronted with such a Chinese policy, would have simply imposed import restrictions. Even if this worked, though, it would be highly unsatisfactory. An import surcharge applied generally, as by President Nixon in 1971, would at least not apply arbitrary biases to the flow of product, spending and income within the economy. But a surcharge applied to China only would be discriminatory, and would penalise US companies sourcing from China on entirely legitimate cost-minimising principles. It would also be extremely unpopular with US consumers, who have gained a lot from low-cost Asian sourcing. Quite possibly, much of the Chinese-sourced goods would find a way round the surcharge, through neighbouring countries' re-exports. And the sight of the US breaching the accepted principles of free trade would be a huge setback for the world economy and development.

In the event, as explained in Chapter 1, the US has found a way of accelerating the reversion to mean of real exchange rates, ie, correction of undue cheapness of Chinese labour and costliness of US labour. Chinese inflation has been mightily stimulated by the excess demand that is intrinsic to an undervalued economy. The effective revaluation of bilateral relative unit labour costs between the US and China was in the region of a 15% annual rate from late 2009 until spring 2011, and is continuing – whether at the same rate or not, time will tell. Over the two years from late-2009 to late-2011, the US could achieve a reduction in its relative labour costs of 25–30% vis-à-vis China. This takes away the chief constraint on US devaluation. The dollar has also been weak against the euro, and various other emerging-market currencies than China. In effect, this means that after the artificially induced boom–bust resulting from the peculiarities of US fiscal policy this year and next, the basis is laid for the economy to advance with net exports in the lead – chiefly, one suspects, through import substitution rather than export growth, given less rosy prospects in most of the rest of the world.

## Baby-boomers will not/cannot retire

The US baby boom started in 1946. The number of people aged 65 was 2.6 million in 2010. With the 1946 cohort hitting 65 this year, there are forecast to be 3.3 million 65-year-olds in 2012, an increase of 700,000 in just two years. This extra 700,000 aged 65 is itself nearly ½% of the labour force. The number of 65-year-olds is projected to continue growing, reaching 3.9 million by 2020. The likelihood is that many, perhaps most, of the baby-boomers will continue working. The current US projections are that the 65–74 age-group participation in the labour force, 25% in 2008, will rise to 30% over the ten years to 2018. This seems too low a projection considering the following factors:

- the increase from 17.7% to 25.1% over the previous decade (to 2008);
- low US savings over the past 15 years, leaving pension funds depleted;
- the crash in house prices and stock market weakness that has reinforced the under-funding of pensions;
- low nominal and real interest rates shrinking investment income and annuity rates;

- the simple reality that rapidly increasing numbers of older people are perfectly able to continue working, are likely to get bored just playing golf, and could dislike the substantial drop in income that is the normal accompaniment of retirement.

As well as a likely underestimate of future participation rates of the over-65s, US labour force projections assume a major erosion of labour-force participation by the 20–24 age group, a (more plausible) continued collapse among 16–19 year-olds, and a minor reduction in the core, 25–54 cohort. Yet in spite of these projections that all appear on the low side, the growth rate of the labour force is forecast to be 0.8% a year from 2008 to 2018, versus 1.1% over the previous ten years. Complicating the issue is the upsurge of 'discouraged workers', who are currently estimated at 1% or so of the labour force (people who do not describe themselves as looking for a job, but who would take work if it were available). The long-term projections disregard such behaviour as cyclical. Certainly, in assessing the impact of labour force supply on employment, labour income and wage rates, discouraged workers are effectively part of the labour force, as they would come back into it if employment conditions improved.

Given the conservatism of the labour force projections, its future growth could be 1% or more. But it seems unlikely that employment growth will even reach, let alone exceed this rate over the next 3–5 years. Unemployment is likely to stay in the 9% region, excluding further major increases in discouraged workers.

The growth of real GDP over the past 20 years since 1990 (a recession year, and sufficiently similar point in the cycle to now) has been 2.5% a year, of which 0.9% has been jobs growth and 1.7% output/head (Table 1). (The numbers do not add up, because

Table 1 **US growth of GDP, jobs and productivity**

| % change per year | 2010/1990 | 2001/1990 | 2010/2001 |
|---|---|---|---|
| Real GDP | 2.5% | 3.2% | 1.7% |
| Jobs | 0.9% | 1.7% | –0.2% |
| Output/employee | 1.7% | 1.5% | 1.9% |

of rounding differences.) But the data from 1990 to 2001 (inter-vening recession) were 3.2% for GDP, 1.7% for jobs and 1.5% for output/employee. In the subsequent nine years, ie, the most recent cycle, it was 1.7% for GDP, minus 0.2% for jobs and 1.9% for output/employee.

Fairly strong growth of productivity is likely to continue, though slower than in the ten years to 2005, when it was power-fully enhanced by adoption of high-tech. The best measure of productivity growth is over 7½ years, as that has been the length of the cycle in recent decades, and its growth is highly sensitive to the cycle over shorter periods. The growth of output per worker-hour in non-farm business on this measure peaked at nearly 3½% in the 7½ years ending 2004, but has been steady at 2–2¼% for the past two years, a good rate for a poor economic cycle. Allow-ing for reduction of this rate by one fifth as productivity growth is minimal in the government sector (one fifth of employment), it is close to 1¾% for the whole economy, which probably implies 1¼–1½% for output per worker, allowing for shorter weekly hours worked over time.

So jobs growth to match labour force growth of 1% or more would require 2½% annual GDP growth. This is likely to be the upper limit of what is achievable, for both supply-side and demand-side reasons. Conventional statistical analysis of poten-tial growth suggests trend growth came down below 2½% in the

2003–04 period and is now well below. The US supply side since 2006 has been harmed by the collapse of housing and real estate services, neither of which is likely to restore its boom-time fortunes in the foreseeable future, and by the probably indefinite downsizing of banks and other financial services.

The credit boom was fundamental to the expansion of financial value-added as a share of GDP. In the five years to 2007, for every $1 growth in US (nominal) GDP the incremental private-sector non-financial debt was $2.50, and total non-financial debt (including government) $3.30. Yet over the period since 2007, private credit, the chief driver of financial activity and off which is festooned the network of swaps, foreign-exchange deals, etc, that make up much of the derivatives market, has been static to declining. How many bankers do you need to lend no more money? For the time being interest margins (the difference between the rates banks borrow and lend at) have been swollen by the crisis and the resulting new awareness of credit risk; also by the need to rebuild capital after the losses in the crash. But over time, the flow of profit will enhance capital, while the lack of growth in loan volume will sharpen competition for what business there is. This should erode interest-rate margins and banking value-added, meaning the shrinkage of the financial industry has a long way to go.

The pattern of growth has been for higher-value activities to do well, but lower-value jobs to go abroad. No amount of devaluation within reason is going to make the lower end of the US labour force competitive with the potential productivity/wage-cost balance of emerging economies. Supply-side factors therefore seem to favour continued good productivity growth in the US (by comparison with Europe and Japan) but little likelihood of jobs growth ahead of labour-force growth – meaning unemployment probably staying in the 9% region (after a dip during 2011 and then a new upswing in the slowdown forecast for 2012). The risks of poor employment growth will be increased if the current focus of government spending cuts is continued. These are chiefly cuts in infrastructure, education and help for disadvantaged families, whose children are the largest reservoir of underutilised US talent, with preservation of the social-security and Medicare entitlements of aging baby-boomers, who, of course, more consistently turn up to vote in elections. This pattern means future supply-side strength is being sacrificed on the altar of entitlements.

The normal demand-side contribution to rebalancing towards new growth sectors is that devaluation with relatively tight fiscal policy would shift demand away from government and/or consumer spending to sectors of US comparative advantage internationally. But the scope for this will be less than in a normal devaluation-plus-belt-tightening episode. The chief reason arises from the fact that the rest of the world has depended for much of the half-century since the 1950s on export-led growth made possible by US readiness to run progressively larger overseas deficits. But it is precisely the nature of the US potential recovery that it will involve lesser net imports. That is the whole point of the need for devaluation, which is now being achieved in relative labour-cost terms. In Chapters 3 and 4, the consequences of this for China are detailed. This means the export-led game is largely over for Pacific Asia, and that in turn means a much lesser flow of easy income in commodity countries. Meanwhile, Chapters 5 and 6 detail the shambles in Europe that presages a decade of stagnation there.

Weakness in Pacific Asia and Europe suggests that the benefits of devaluation for exports will be less than might be hoped. These will be affected heavily by world trade growth, which in turn will be hurt by the habit of world growth depending on US growth and imports, when for current American purposes it needs to be the other way round. In a disappointing world economy, the benefits of US devaluation will therefore have to be concentrated on import substitution. Given the low level of manufacturing output as a share of US output, there is plenty of scope for this, but the absence of great hopes for exports is bound to be an inhibition on medium-term growth.

Aside from these general points, reasons for expecting only moderate medium-term growth include the demand and savings consequences of the demographics themselves, and the budget retrenchment already mentioned.

A major factor arguing for stronger than expected labour force participation of over-65 baby-boomers is their lack of adequate pension funding, meaning a large drop in income on retirement. It follows that their social security receipts, due from age 66, could be largely saved, or deferred: if saved, the short-term recent decline of the personal savings rate is likely to be reversed in favour of renewal of the upward shift in evidence until mid-2010; or, if deferred, the flow of income will simply fall short. In a more general sense, the recent QE2-related upsurge of risk-asset prices and fall in savings look like a temporary reversion to pre-2007-style denial of the underlying weakness of household balance sheets. The personal sector has debt that has come well back from its peak of 129% of disposable income towards what we calculate to be a long-term sustainable ratio of 110%. (See Appendix 1 for the analysis of sustainable debt ratios.) In addition, the increasing longevity of the now quite aged baby-boomers makes necessary (or at least desirable) a mixture of longer working lives and higher savings, of which it is unlikely to be all the former and none of the latter.

This tendency of the savings rate to rise may be reinforced in its impact on the consumer spending share of GDP by a weakening ratio of labour income. Both the high rate of unemployment, and the general point that an excess supply of labour ought to lower its relative price, point this way. In particular, the ten-year labour force projections involving sharp falls in labour force participation for under-25s, as well as more modest falls all the way up to age 54, may well not be solely the result of unforced preferences: aging baby-boomers hanging onto their jobs may make it harder for the young to get started in employment. This potentially creates downward pressure on wages and salaries relative to the overall flow of income.

If consumer spending is to grow more slowly than GDP, as seems likely, what element of demand will rise as a share of GDP? While weakness of labour income implies improved underlying margins, slow consumption growth combined with government spending cuts suggest that business cap-ex is unlikely to progress much faster than GDP, though a more competitive real effective exchange rate should create opportunities. Housing investment too could remain weak, with the overhang of past overinvestment still largely in place. It follows that there is only one sector of demand left that can show a significant increase: net exports. In other words, the implications of US demographics over the next five years, combined with government spending austerity, are falling net imports.

At some stage in 2012, owing to the boom–bust policy mechanism that has been put in place, imports could simply fall in response to growth itself heading towards, if not below, zero – the much discussed 'double-dip'. But over the medium term, export competitiveness and, more importantly, import substitution should prevail, aided by superior US productivity growth as well as relative labour cost restraint. If, as seems likely, present boom conditions in energy and metal prices ease off, the US may also gain net income from improved terms of trade (export versus import prices) especially if food prices remain strong – America being the world's largest agricultural exporter.

## Budget balancing turns overseas deficit to surplus

When it comes to budget austerity itself, the scale of the cuts could be severe. US government sector revenues – at all levels, federal, state, local, social security, etc – were some 32% of GDP in 2010 (see Figure 6 on p. 37). Suppose real GDP advances by 12–13% over the next five years and revenues remain the same as a percentage of GDP, then reduction of the deficit to 3–4% of GDP requires cutting spending from its current 42% of GDP to 35–36% (3–4% above the revenue level) of a GDP that will be 112–113% of current levels. This 35–36% ratio to a future real GDP up one eighth (12–13%) in real terms is 40% of current GDP. But this year, total public outlays are set at some 42% of GDP. So to get it down to the required level requires cuts of more than 1% in real government spending (nearly ½% of GDP each year) for five successive years. Yet many programmes are virtually untouchable, eg, social security, debt interest, Medicare, Medicaid, and increasing in real terms. Others, such as defence spending, are – or have been – 'sacred cows', even (or especially) to Republican deficit-hawks.

Any programme of general spending cuts will have to run the gauntlet of special interest lobbying – in a country where limits on lobbies' political contributions are now unconstitutional – and the local interests of a plethora of Congress people. Some progress will be made – and allowing the Bush tax cuts to lapse, at least partially, when they come up for renewal again in two years' time may yield some extra tax revenue. But the achievement of deficit reduction to 3–4% of GDP must be in doubt, even over a five-year timescale, in the absence of what now seems like a very un-American readiness to accept general tax increases. (Perhaps this is what lies behind the recent talk of tax 'reform', which might raise revenue by broadening the tax base without raising rates, as was done by President Reagan in 1986.)

The implications of budget austerity for the flows of funds supports the argument that net imports will be reduced. Currently, the 10% government deficit is offset by private savings in excess of private investment equal to 7% of GDP, leaving a 3%-plus overseas deficit. Within the private sector, households are saving about 4% of GDP (5½–6% of their disposable income), which housing investment of 2–2½% reduces to a notional household surplus of close to 2%. The remaining 5%-plus of private surplus is the excess of business saving (retained profits plus depreciation) over capital spending and inventory accumulation. But household saving is likely to increase, and housing investment is not, so the household balance is heading *upward* from 2% towards 3% or more. Meanwhile, the business sector could see improving margins (as labour income is restrained by demographic over-supply) while its capital spending is hardly likely to be booming in the face of relatively slow economic growth, though a 'hard landing' for the US economy next year will cut business profits in the short term. Taking these points together, current and prospective behaviour patterns suggest a major decline in the private sector's 7%-plus surplus is unlikely.

All this means that if the budget deficit is brought down much more than half-way from its current 10% of GDP to a target of 3–4% it could be equal to or less than the private surplus, implying an overseas surplus – a far cry from recent deficits. Nor is this an unlikely result of a combination of ongoing need for household debt deleverage, strong business margins and government budget retrenchment.

For government debt, the arithmetic is discouraging, if less so than for most other deficit countries after the 'Great Recession'. Net US government debt was 65% of GDP at end-2010 (gross debt being 92%) including state and local as well as federal, but excluding a host of contingent obligations such as Fannie Mae and Freddie Mac – not to say, implicitly, as became clear in the financial crisis, the entire financial sector, whose inclusion would double the gross ratio. If real GDP in five years is up 12–13%, nominal GDP could be up 20%. If the deficit averages 7–8% of GDP over those years (a middling assumption) then net debt will reach 90% of GDP, with gross debt well over 100%. As nominal GDP growth could be 4% and the deficit ratio still above 4% by then, the debt ratio would still be rising. This is not a disaster, but shows the cost of rebalancing the economy and its private sector balance sheets. While not a disaster, such a level of debt is wildly unpopular, and will become more so as the ratio rises.

In all of this analysis, the inflation problem that receives a lot of attention fails to emerge on any large scale. The chief reason is that the US economy can be expected to remain underemployed and the inflationary impact of QE2 is mostly felt in China – plus the other countries artificially holding down their exchange rates, eg, Germany and Brazil. Lombard Street Research's estimate is that slack in the economy was down to 1½% of GDP in early 2011, much less than would normally be associated with unemployment of about 9%. The growth expected late in 2011 could eliminate this slack – the burst of investment in the second half could even generate an extremely temporary positive output gap, ie, overheating, but giving way to output below trend again next year as the investment boom is followed by relapse.

Using the assumption that oil prices remain unchanged as China wrestles down its inflation rate, but that non-oil import prices continue to rise quite fast (China again) CPI inflation is likely to stay in the 2–3% region this year, and could then ease down in 2012's slowdown. Core inflation (excluding food and energy) could peak close to 2% at the end of the year and early 2012 before then falling back again toward the zero core inflation that is always threatened by the combination of deleverage and budget restraint. This forecast of contained inflation and then renewed deflation risk is reinforced by the actual decline of unit labour costs over most of the past three years, and probable continued wage and salary restraint over the medium term, owing to buoyant labour force growth and still-high unemployment.

The outlook described here is not a particularly happy one in absolute terms, given forecast unemployment remaining close to 9% or so for several years, with a 'feel-bad' recovery that passes consumers by. But it does entail a relatively full US rebalancing, both financially and economically. Moreover, relative to other countries, especially China, Pacific Asia generally, Europe, and 'commodity countries', US prospects are substantially better than is generally thought. Obviously, China, however much its growth trend may be cut, can be expected to grow faster than the US, but on the forecast in the following two chapters its economy would take another 20 years to equal that of the US, at which point its people's average income would only be one quarter of America's. So this forecast implies at least another quarter-century of US global economic dominance, especially given the potential economic eclipse of Europe.

# 3

# China's export-led growth model breaks down

China's miraculous growth machine has produced outstanding results, but they were only made possible by good fortune abroad. After Mao, the Chinese people had nothing but brawn, brains and sheer determination to succeed. By opening its economy to the world in 1978, much like Japan did after the Korean War, China kick-started its fast growth. The first two decades of reform saw substantial productivity gains from disbanding agricultural communes and shifting labour from agriculture to low-end manufacturing and processing, mostly for export. The moment export incomes started to rise in the 1980s, savings also rose. Savings are especially vital for a developing economy as they provide the financial resources needed for heavy investment in factories, machines, roads, homes, schools and hospitals, permitting income catch-up.

The first two decades of China's miraculous growth era saw dramatic change, but catching up on the developed world was easy because China started off so poor. China became a formidable export machine thanks to a huge pool of extraordinarily cheap labour and opening its market to foreign direct investment and know-how. Increasing the amount of capital at workers' disposal even by a small amount produced huge gains in productivity. And the more China saved and invested, the faster incomes grew and the easier it became to save more. This was the virtuous cycle that the thrifty Chinese enjoyed. But savings can turn from good into bad. Investment is derived demand. Its ultimate justification is consumption and export growth. The more Chinese people saved out of their income, the lesser proportion they spent on clothes, phones, televisions and cars. Saving more to invest more is a dead end when there is no increase in the desire and/or ability to consume more or export more.

China entered its malign savings phase in the mid-1990s. Consumption as a share of income had been in decline until then, but the share of exports rose fast. The rest of the world did not object to China carving out larger chunks of the global trade pie. For all the growth in the country's exports, only in 1993 did China's share of world trade reach its pre-1939 peak. Then between 1994 and 2000 the share of exports in income stagnated. China saw inflation spiral out of control in 1993–95. Policymakers tightened the economy's monetary belt and embarked on the Herculean task of dismantling the huge, but mostly moribund, state-owned industrial sector. As a result, the national savings rate declined, but the investment rate fell faster to produce a sizable current account surplus. But when in 1997 the Asian financial crisis hit, although China's closed capital account prevented financial contagion, the demand shock from the collapse in exports was substantial.

Beijing's response was a huge stimulus package aimed at boosting domestic demand. But the real *coup* for China was joining the World Trade Organisation (WTO) in 2001. Most major countries have accepted free trade in goods and services and made great progress in its implementation, with clear exclusions, notably agriculture. Lured by the prospect of entering China's potentially huge domestic market, the rest of the world opened up its markets fully to China. China's export-led growth received a supersonic boost. Exports surged from 20% of GDP in 2001 to 35% in 2007. China's ability to industrialise at breakneck speed has driven supply, but WTO membership was crucial in providing the foreign markets for China's surplus products. While China has fast become the world's manufacturing powerhouse, the emergence of the Chinese consumer has remained a chimera.

Throughout the recent third decade of miraculous growth, China's excessive savings ballooned. In fact the national savings rate, comprising the saving of households, firms and the government, shot up to an unprecedented 54% of GDP in 2010, while the household consumption rate fell to 34% of GDP, a record low even for a developing economy. Such high savings could not be invested profitably in the domestic economy. In China's semi-command economy they have no need to be. In China, private and state-owned firms alike are not driven by profitability. Private entrepreneurs are focused entirely on the short term, exploiting arbitrage opportunities with little regard for strategic planning. No wonder the production of fake goods is so widespread. State-owned 'national champions' appear profitable but enjoy a raft of subsidies or monopoly positions.

The most important subsidy is access to mispriced cheap loans. The bulk of China's savings are held in the state-owned banks, which lend primarily to state-owned firms or investment vehicles set up by local governments to avoid a ban on direct bank borrowing. China's policymakers control the direction, amount and cost of loans, keeping borrowing interest rates low. If state firms cannot pay their debts, new loans are dished out to keep them going. Thus the financial sustainability of past investment binges is not undermined during economic downturns. Banks accumulate bad loans. But the expectation is that strong output growth will shrink them away over time. Banks may be insolvent, but they are not illiquid. As long as the closed exchange controls prevent capital outflows, domestic savings must stay at home, mostly deposited with state banks. Steadily rising bank deposits supply new loans for old, and state companies never default. Companies can't run out of cash, so they never go bust. Banks never run out of cash and they can't go bust. Liquidity hides insolvency.

China is incredibly good at wasting savings through misallocating investment. It can either waste its savings domestically or abroad. In the first half of the last decade domestic savings mostly went into a massive domestic investment boom. There was a huge build-up of excess capacity, especially in the manufacturing sector. While trade flows were liberalised, Beijing kept its exchange rate fixed to the dollar and the capital account closed. Unsurprisingly, overinvestment and a pegged currency resulted in the world being flooded with made-in-China manufactured goods, whose prices kept falling fast. Later, energy and commodity prices surged on the world market as Chinese production was extremely inefficient in its use of resources. But this was not reflected in the price of manufacturing goods because Beijing does not allow domestic energy prices to be set by the market. Ultimately, China could not escape the business cycle. By 2004 it had run into severe energy and transport shortages, which curbed its investment frenzy. Over the next two years domestic demand growth slowed significantly.

China was still saving excessively, but now it had to find

another channel to waste its huge and rising savings – this time exporting them to the Americans. China's current account surplus surged, dwarfing its previous increase. The yuan–dollar peg had also forced Japan and the Asian Tigers, which had excess savings for their own reasons, to manage their currencies against the US dollar, as these economies were scared of being 'hollowed out' even further by China. Asian official capital outflows poured into low-risk, low-yielding dollar assets, bringing yields down and stoking America's consumer boom, which itself fuelled China's export-led growth machine. But the Goldilocks relationship was broken down once the private sector in the US exhausted its ability to build up debt and the excesses in the housing and financial sectors became visible, triggering the seize-up of global liquidity and the near-collapse of the global financial system.

Central banks and regulators across the world fell seriously behind the curve by failing to grasp the profound global changes at play. Their focus remained firmly at home. Regulators ignored the potential dangers of the surge in bank disintermediation. Central bankers failed to realise how manufacturing prices were set globally; where the 'conundrum' of low bond yields came from; why the surge in energy prices did not translate into higher domestic wage inflation. Importantly, they did not pay attention to money and asset price developments, and, crucially, private sector debt levels relative to income. The harbingers of the global overheating and the crescendo of the build-up of debt excesses that began in 2006 came in the form of above-trend broad money and credit growth and asset price inflation.

The Chinese authorities also made a mistake. They allowed some appreciation of the yuan versus the US dollar, but not enough. And in effective exchange rate terms the yuan was up by a lot less, as Beijing took advantage of the stronger euro. Beijing thought the yuan–dollar peg was serving China well because it kept international influences at bay, but policymakers failed to realise that China had become too big and could no longer be immune to global developments. China could not avoid the consequences of the collapse in global trade and the 'Great Recession'. In the event, its own recession at the end of 2008 was one of the most severe in the world.

Global problems needed a global solution. But this appears beyond the powers of policymakers on either side of the saver–borrower divide, suggesting that each country fends for itself. Three years on from the financial crisis, the global status quo has not changed. America is still borrowing excessively, but this time the public sector is doing the heavy lifting. China continues to save excessively and rely on exports and investment to pull its economy forward.

China and America were happy to party together, but each economy is recovering from the hangover alone. Much like Japan in the 1960s, China since 1994, but even more so since 2001 was operating in a benign world trade environment. Its miraculous growth years have been the result of unusually favourable domestic and international circumstances. The achievements of those years should not be belittled, but they were the product of a unique set of circumstances which are no longer there.

The financial crisis marks a major turning point for China's export and investment led catch-up growth model. The workout of the global financial imbalances is set to be prolonged and to weigh on global growth for years. The rest of the world will no longer tolerate China's continual grabbing of market share and refusal to budge on the currency. (Indeed, once dominance of an industry is achieved, little share remains to be grabbed.) The external demand shock has undermined the sustainability of China's exorbitant investment rate. China's potential growth rate could well halve to 5% during this decade. The greatest problem policymakers have to contend with is coming to terms with the social and political consequences of much slower growth.

## China's scope for catch-up growth curtailed by its size

Some believe China still has substantial scope for catch-up growth because its average standard of living is still only 14% of America's at purchasing power parity (PPP) – that is, with goods and services output valued at US prices, instead of Chinese. By contrast, after Japan's comparable near-10% growth phase ending in the mid-1970s, its average was over 70% of America's. So China ought still to have great potential for catch-up growth by transferring existing technology to equip its cheaper labour force.

Yes it has, but no it hasn't. It can physically raise production, but won't do so unless it can sell the extra products. When it can no longer sell more abroad, it can only grow by selling more at home. That is the problem. The snag is China's sheer size. This has produced a meteoric rise to over 13% of world GDP at PPP basis – reflecting the compound of nearly one-seventh of the US standard of living with over four times its population. China is the world's second largest economy. In 2011 China surpassed the US as the largest global manufacturer, accounting for close to 20% of the total. In 2010 China was already the largest exporter of manufactured goods. Little countries can go on capturing shares in big world markets until their income per head catches up. Big countries cannot unless they make world markets commensurately bigger. Either their share in world consumption must grow or their share in world production will stop growing.

China's output is concentrated in the low value-added, low-skilled assembly end of industrial processes, with the high-value, sophisticated parts to be assembled still to a large degree sourced from Japan, South Korea and Taiwan. As a result, China already both dominates and has saturated global output and capacity in many low-value added industries. In 2008 China accounted for 43% of the global real value-added in textiles, 39% of wearing apparel, 43% of leather and footwear, and 28% of electrical machinery and apparatus. China has the capacity to supply nearly 80% of world demand for air conditioners and mobile phones. Once it establishes a dominant position in supplying a product, growth can proceed only at the pace of world demand.

So, although in relative income-per-capita terms China still has plenty of catch-up potential, in absolute terms it is already over 60% of the US in PPP GDP, twice Japan's 1970s ratio. If the growth model is unchanged, China's huge size means that to maintain the high growth rates of the past the economy needs to move up the value-added chain fast by grabbing even more market share. But put simply, whatever it does, China cannot expect to make all the world's manufacturing goods. The world is not big enough to accommodate a pure rise up the value-added chain. But this constraint to catch-up growth in PPP terms or in other words in real terms does not mean that the scope for China's depressed nominal income levels to catch up is constrained. But for that adjustment to proceed without a major disruption to China's advance, the growth model still needs to be changed.

## China's high savings rate key for its growth model

A Martian was sent to Earth to study America's and China's financial systems. He went to New York and was impressed by the size of the financial industry. He then beamed himself to Beijing and saw a much smaller financial sector. Upon return to Mars he declared his conclusion to be that in the US people save a lot, but in China they save very little. He was both right and wrong. Older Americans do save a lot. But they also lend to the young who borrow and spend – hence the large financial industry, doing the intermediation of savings. But in aggregate savings are low. Our Martian, however, was wrong to infer from the much smaller financial sector that the Chinese people, firms and state save too little.

'China is different' is a mantra often repeated to justify the expectation of its unabated fast future expansion. Indeed China's economic model is unique, but unravelling how its economy works will be much more instructive in trying to anticipate the future than blind belief in a miraculous growth machine. After all the same epithet was used for Japan, whose success in rebuilding its economy and raising the living standard of its population was undeniable. Yet its growth machine progressively lost its impetus after years of heady near-10% growth rates to go through a turbulent couple of decades in the 1970s and 1980s, which saw the economy's growth rate halve. Japan's growth machine eventually spluttered after its massive property and equity market bubble burst in the late-1980s to remain depressed in the next two decades with no sign of revival on the horizon. A natural parallel exists with Japan's experience, which is illuminating as much in its differences in comparison to China's as it is in its similarities.

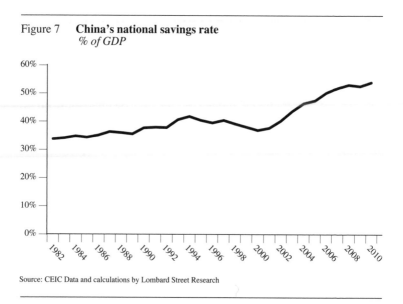

Figure 7    **China's national savings rate**
            *% of GDP*

Source: CEIC Data and calculations by Lombard Street Research

China and Japan share one similarity which has been crucial in underpinning their respective growth machines. The moment output and incomes started to rise in both Japan in the 1950s and China in the 1980s, savings also rose. Between the early 1950s and 1970 Japanese gross national savings rose to a peak of 40% of gross national incomes (roughly equal to GDP). In China, between the early 1980s and 2010 the comparable savings rate climbed to a peak of 54% (Figure 7).

Savings are vital for an underdeveloped economy, which needs to increase its industrial capital stock to boost productivity and output growth. Its often fast growing population also requires a fast expansion in its infrastructure. People demand better roads, trains, airports, hospitals, schools and homes. Both Japan's and China's industrialisation were helped enormously by the ability to finance fast growth with domestic savings, thus avoiding the vicious circle of balance of payments and public debt crises that plagued the Latin American economies whose inadequate savings pushed them into heavy foreign borrowing.

## China's banks key to explaining the high savings rate

China's financial sector holds the key in explaining its high national savings rate. At the heart of the financial sector and the Chinese semi-command economy lies its banking sector. Banks do the bulk of the intermediation of domestic savings, but the sector is dominated by the big four state-owned banks, who hold over half the domestic deposits. As explained above, their lending is not done according to market principles, in other words in search of higher return after a proper credit risk assessment. Actually, China has made a lot of progress improving banks' ability to assess credit risk, implementing proper lending practices. The problem is that the authorities remain all too ready to override these practices to provide cheap credit when and where it suits their objectives. It is an economy in transition from command to market. It easily slips back to command when thought necessary.

Over the years the banking sector has primarily served the needs of the state sector. The central and local governments were allowed to borrow directly from banks until rapid monetisation of the budget deficit led to yet another bout of high inflation in the early 1990s. Direct bank lending to the government was banned in 1994. But the bulk of bank lending since then, about two thirds, has gone to state-owned firms or local government special financing vehicles, used to avoid the ban on direct bank borrowing. Private firms and households have been starved of bank finance.

During each credit-fuelled economic boom banks build up bad debts. In 1999 state banks dumped 1.4 trillion yuan of bad loans into special asset management companies and in 2005 another 1.2 trillion yuan. Given the lack of transparency it is difficult to judge how big the current banks' bad loan problem is. Official estimates relating just to the loans given to the special financing vehicles suggest as much as another 2 to 3 trillion yuan may need to be removed from banks' balance sheets. It is fair to say that the massive explosion in Chinese credit during 2009 and 2010 in the context of deficient global demand is likely to have burdened state banks with a substantial amount of bad debts.

Chinese banks may be *de facto* insolvent, but they never need be *de jure* declared so. The government can always sweep bad loans under the carpet. If it does not take them on directly, it can move them to asset management companies. In 2009 such bail-out companies' funding was rolled over for another ten years, giving time for bad assets to become good again or at least preventing losses from being realised for a while. Losses on bad bank loans did not exist in the fully command economy. Profits were irrelevant, a capitalist accounting concept. The transition towards a market economy created the recognition of bad loans without eliminating the state sector's need for them. China's policymakers still control the direction, amount and cost of most loans, keeping borrowing interest rates low. Exchange controls preventing capital outflows are the linchpin of this system. Without them household deposits could seek greater returns elsewhere. Bank deposit growth would slow. Roll-over and new lending would need to be curtailed. State companies could face liquidity problems bringing in their wake revelation of insolvencies. The partial transition from command to a market financial system, as Japan discovered, means each liberalisation demands the next or must be rolled back. Standing still is not an option.

Beijing's strategy so far has been not to realise the losses on the bad loans that have been accumulated while the economy industrialised fast. The expectation has been that over time strong growth will shrink the bad debts away. The problem is that bad debts continue to mount every time growth slows, while there is understandably little political resolve to release state control of the banking system and allow it to function according to market principles. This would impose an intolerable squeeze on the state sector, which is shrinking by not growing in a high-growth economy, but as yet has not withered away. The longer the economy operates in this manner, the higher is policymakers' incentive to keep interest rates down. Without such life support some zombie firms will cease to exist. But importantly all investment decisions are taken on the basis of state-mandated cheap finance, inflating both total savings and total (wasteful) investment.

## Inefficient lending behind each sector's saving

The grossly inefficient intermediation of savings is a crucial factor behind China's abnormally high savings rate in all three sectors of the economy: the business sector, the household sector and the government. If excess savings are not consumed by wasteful expenditure (and the saver cheated in the process) incomes and consumption must contract. The government sector is the smallest saver in China, but it has been a major contributor to the rise in

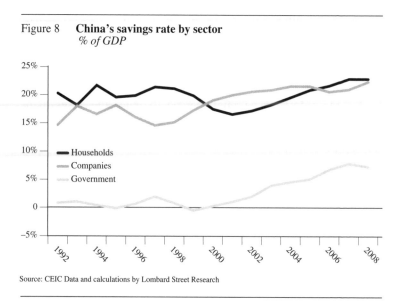

Figure 8    **China's savings rate by sector**
             *% of GDP*

Source: CEIC Data and calculations by Lombard Street Research

national saving in the last decade. Its savings rate was over 10% in 2008, up from 3% in 2000. The business sector savings rate rose during the 1990s to reach 20% of GDP in 2001, but it has since been fairly stable. The household savings rate was stable for most of the 1990s, then fell after the Asian financial crisis, but resumed its mild upward march after 2001 to reach 23% of GDP in 2008 as consumers' propensity to save rose (Figure 8). As already noted, in total, domestic savings have now risen to an unprecedented 54% of national income in 2010.

In the state sector, where firms have ready access to credit, investment has been artificially boosted by low interest rates. Cheap money helps create retained earnings. State companies earn to save and save so they can spend on capital expansion. Meanwhile, private firms have little access to bank credit. As a result, they hoard cash to use for expansion or to hedge against future uncertainties rather than distribute it. There is no culture of distributing dividends. In the state sector it was government policy in the 1990s and for most of the noughties that firms were not required to pay dividends to cushion the impact of the aggressive state-sector restructuring that started in the mid-1990s.

This changed in 2007 when a certain number of state firms were required to pay a mandatory dividend – a further step on the road to a market economy. A small group of the country's biggest companies were required to pay the maximum 10% dividend. Around 100 companies had to pay 5% of profits, and the rest paid nothing at all. In 2011, an additional 1,631 state firms joined the dividend programme, while the dividend payout ratio was raised by 5% for most firms to a total of 15% for some. But even so dividend payout ratios in the state sector in China are well below the 33% average dividend payout ratios that prevail among state-owned firms in other countries.

One of the key elements of China's reforms was to open up its economy to inward foreign direct investment, in contrast to Japan, which did not rely on direct external finance. This sped up the build-up of China's modern capital base, providing not just the necessary finance to the private sector but also transferring much needed know-how. The Chinese, like the Japanese, were still saving every penny in the initial years, but domestic savings were ploughed back mainly into the state sector of the economy. Until China's private sector was able to stand on its two feet, foreign direct investment was vital in providing finance to a nascent but rapidly growing part of the economy.

The government in China may be the smallest saver, but it was the main contributor to the rise in savings during the last decade. The marked increase in government saving largely reflects higher government income. True, high economic growth, corporate restructuring and the 1994 tax reforms played a role in boosting government income. But the key force at play is the fact that the government borrows very little from the Chinese people or abroad, instead using the state banking system to finance its large investment in social infrastructure. This fuels strong growth and strong government revenues, while the government has to pay little interest to finance its gigantic infrastructure investment plans. State-directed bank lending, however, is a liability of the government, even if a hidden one. If it is included in the official estimates of public debt, it will push it much higher. Public sector debt is estimated at around 30% of GDP in 2009, but a sizable chunk of it is actually also held by the banks.

Here lies another difference with Japan which explains why China has seen a much higher national savings rate. In the first stage of Japan's expansion until 1965, under the Dodge plan the government had to balance the budget. In fact initially, far from being allowed to borrow, it had to save, as it needed to repay maturing bonds. The Japanese saved every extra yen which was then devoted to financing corporate expansion. The direct borrowing ban was circumvented to some extent in the Japanese shadow public sector, with the postal savings system used to finance public expenditure. After 1965 the policy of balancing the budget was abandoned and running budget deficits became fashionable. In fact it became a necessity, as the easiest route to battle the problem of excess private sector savings was to move to reduced government savings by means of budget deficits. Instead of the surpluses covering all the public sector investment, the government borrowed from the public to cover part of the cost.

Chinese households are big savers. At 23% of GDP, household

savings are less than half Chinese national savings. But they are approaching a third of disposable income. There are many reasons. Banks lend very little to households. They were allowed to lend for home purchases in 1997. Mortgage borrowing surged from zero to 10% of GDP in 2004. But banks had little expertise with lending to households and had difficulty enforcing foreclosures on delinquent loans. There was no centralised tracking of the credit history of either individuals or firms until 2003. On the other hand, the fact that banks were mainly state-owned had an impact on people's behaviour. Banks enjoyed the explicit deposit insurance that came with state ownership. But much in the same way that people felt their savings were secure in the state-owned banks, they also considered borrowing from the state-owned banks as laying their hands on money that was rightfully theirs. There is certainly no cultural stigma attached to defaulting on a loan as there is in other parts of Asia. As a result, the bulk of these mortgage loans quickly turned sour and banks halted their expansion. Mortgage borrowing languished for five years afterwards, despite expectations of China moving towards consumer-driven growth.

The banks' focus on financing state-directed investment means the young cannot borrow from the old, so they have to save a lot. In the last decade China's economy was booming and incomes growing, but instead of consuming more, households were actually saving an increasing proportion of the higher income they were earning. This seems counterintuitive, but it makes sense when banks lend primarily to firms. As people's incomes rose, they started to covet the big ticket items such as cars and houses. They could not borrow to buy them, so they had to save more.

The household sector gets a double whammy. Two-thirds of

household financial assets are in interest bearing deposits, so artificially low interest rates mean artificially low household income.
Household bank deposits earn very little. The real interest rate
on one-year household deposits averaged 0.6% a year in the last
decade. But bank deposits are the safe option that the Chinese
have been used to for years. The meagre rate of increase on their
real wealth is a crucial reason behind the Chinese high savings.

Households have few options for investing their wealth. Individuals cannot buy financial assets outside of China. Beijing
created the Qualified Domestic Institutional Investor scheme in
2006, which allows institutional money to flow out of China, but
the outflows are minimal for now. In 2009 China's non-govern-
ment foreign security assets amounted to 243 billion US dollars.
In the US the corresponding figure was 17 times bigger. As the
development of China's securities markets deepened, the domestic stock market began to attract a larger part of households'
wealth. But so far the experience of the Chinese people has been
that of paltry returns for years, followed by a rapid surge in 2006
and 2007, equally swiftly followed by a slump in 2008. This is
unlikely to convince people of the value of domestic equities as
a long-term investment. The stock market lacks transparency
and the value of equities is often altered at the whim of arbitrary
administrative interference. And with the government not issuing
that much debt, there is little supply of another risk-free alternative to bank deposits.

## Corporate restructuring also behind the savings glut

Keeping interest rates low favours the corporate sector over the household sector in the distribution of national income. The household savings rate as a share of household disposable income as opposed to GDP has risen much faster since 2000 as household disposable income fell as a share of GDP. The fall in household investment income played a role, but the main reason was the declining share of labour income in the economy.

Until 2004 the economy was still going through massive corporate restructuring with the size of the state sector shrinking. This led to large-scale labour retrenchment, which combined with the continued influx of rural migrants to undermine labour's bargaining power, as China had a seemingly limitless pool of low-skilled workers. By the middle of the decade the pace of state sector shrinkage abated. But by then China's corporate sector actually ran into its cyclical buffers, experiencing significant energy and transport shortages, which pared back its investment binge. It was the turn of the private sector to get its act together and restructure aggressively, cutting labour costs. There was also a sustained drive to improve the performance of the big state-owned companies that were intended to stay in government hands.

So, labour costs were held down and better corporate performance did not translate into improved household incomes. Wage growth in the manufacturing sector is likely to have undershot productivity growth. This is also why there has been little relative service price inflation in China, which is a benign form of inflation by which the benefits from rising productivity in manufacturing are shared with workers in other industries and services.

Excess labour supply amid the massive corporate restructuring and continued rural–urban migration not only led to the declining share of labour income, but also contributed to the increase in the households' desire to save. China's state sector employees not only enjoyed life-long job security, but also benefited from generous pension provisions. The progressive loss of that job security and less generous pension provisions for a large part of the workforce during 1997–2005 was a major factor behind increased insecurity and the rising household savings rate. Working in the state sector in China used to resemble Japan's lifetime employment system, but the role of the lifetime employment system in Japan did not start to diminish until after the economy lost most of its growth momentum in the 1990s.

## The one-child policy and urbanisation

China's one-child policy and urbanisation also partly explain high savings. The role of the family is rapidly diminishing. The one-child policy, announced in 1978 came into force in 1979. It was introduced when the birth rate had soared. From 1960 to 1975 the net reproduction rate exceeded two – on average a woman during child-bearing age had more than two daughters. The total fertility rate, including sons, was around five. The population was doubling about every 35 years. Something had to be done. The one-child policy was draconian. There were exceptions: rural dwellers and initially families without a son could have another chance.

The result was dramatic. The net reproduction rate fell to under one and the total fertility rate to under two. The population would consequently peak and then decline at an accelerating rate. If continued for 100 years the family as such would cease to exist. For the past three decades, brothers and sisters have been abolished. Cousins, uncles, aunts, nieces and nephews will now follow. If not life-threatening, the policy was family threatening. It has now been eased. Two single children who wed can have two children. Nonetheless the social ramifications are immense. It increases both single children and their parents desire to save. Children worry about providing for their parents, while the parents worry about providing for themselves.

Urbanisation has also put a strain on family ties. China's urbanisation really kicked off at the start of the last decade. Between 2000 and 2010 the Population Census estimates that about 117 million rural residents moved to the city. In 2010 there were around 221 million rural migrants working in the cities. These figures could understate the true scale of rural–urban migration. And it is massive – even taking these numbers over 16% of the population migrated from country to town.

But while rural migrants flocked to the cities, China did nothing to change the discriminatory nature of its household registration system known as *hukou*. A decade after the Communist Party came to power, the *hukou* system was officially promulgated, although residency permits dated back to ancient China. Under *hukou* a person inherits the household registration of their mother. Individuals were broadly categorised as either rural or urban *hukou* holders, with urban residents enjoying a range of privileges while rural residents were treated as second-rate citizens. Registration was tied to a complex set of migration restriction, basically prohibiting migration upwards to an urban *hukou*. Urban *hukou* holders could move to a smaller city or a village or villagers could move from one village to another. But to change a rural *hukou* to an urban *hukou* was extremely hard. Over the years millions of urban residents were mobilised to leave and settle in smaller cities or villages, and they could no longer return to their places of birth.

Before China's economic reforms, the *hukou* system was enforced stringently. After 1978, the authorities were less strict and migration began, driven by economic progress. But initially those migrants were akin to illegal immigrants. They were on the fringes of urban society, living in squalor, working long hours, unable to visit home or bring their families with them and dreaming of making enough money to return to the countryside. Their living conditions remain depressing, recently brought to the forefront by the series of suicides at the Foxcon's factories. The system was relaxed in the mid-1990s when rural *hukou* holders were allowed to buy residency permits, so they can work legally, with fees gradually coming down. Later the *hukou* could also be inherited through either parent. Yet the *hukou* system, which still attributes certain rights and obligations according to the place of birth not residence, has persisted throughout the 30 years of China's miraculous growth.

Survey data suggests that rural migrants saw a substantial increase in their incomes as a result of finding higher paid industry jobs. There is also evidence that they have a much higher savings rate because of their disadvantaged *hukou* status. In 2007 the urban savings rate as a percent of disposable income in Guangzhou was 15.6% and in Shenzhen 27.5%. The rural migrant savings rate as a percent of total income was 41% in Guangzhou and 42% in Shenzhen. The rural migrant has had little access to welfare benefits, proper medical care and free education. An urban *hukou* entitles its holder to free or low-cost basic education. That privilege is denied to the rural migrant and rural *hukou* holder. One recent survey found that when asked which were the top two reasons for saving, rural migrants pointed to education (40%), followed by savings to build houses in home villages (32%) and saving for illness and other misfortunes (28.5%).

Rural–urban migration has weakened family links, which is also likely to have led to a higher savings rate. Taking care of parents is part of Chinese culture, but migration has taken its toll on filial duties. China is now even considering making it a legal duty for people to visit their aged parents. Under a draft legal amendment, elderly people could go to court to claim their right to be physically and mentally looked after by their children.

An important feature of China's urbanisation has been the geographical expansion of cities. This has also affected national savings. Lots of people became urbanised without moving. Growing towns gobbled up the countryside. There was a large increase in the number of cities and the land existing cities claimed. Even though more and more Chinese people have become urban residents, the population density of the Chinese cities has remained low, constant over time, or even declining. The turn of the century also saw a change in this type of urbanisation. The average size of cities increased by some 60% between 1996 and 2004. Urbanisation is supposed to be economically beneficial not just because it moves people from low-productivity agriculture to higher productivity manufacturing, but because it also makes production more efficient by creating clusters of economic activity. And there has been a fair amount of this in China, but a key part has been state mandated expansion of city boundaries, within which there could also be many people doing agricultural work.

The government has been a major beneficiary from the cities' geographical expansion. In communist China all the land is owned by local government. In 1994 China changed its tax system to ensure a boost of central government revenues, which had plummeted during the reform years. Most of the taxes collected locally were sent to the central coffers. Local governments had to rely on a system of tax rebates which left them scrambling for cash. This not only meant that the provision of services by the local governments deteriorated, but also resulted in local governments using land sales to fund their infrastructure spending spree. Local governments' success is judged on the economic growth of the region, which incentivises local politicians to go for growth. The 1994 tax reforms and the 1998 housing reforms which phased out the previous system of the state providing all urban housing are likely to explain the massive geographical expansion of cities in China, as more and more land was sold for real estate development. The resulting increase in land sales boosted government revenues, which partly explains the surge in the government's savings rate that has occurred since 2000.

## China's savings turned toxic

Japan's benign savings phase lasted until the mid-60s. After the 1965 recession, savings rose faster than investment and persistently exceeded the amount needed to finance it. The savings rate reached a peak of nearly 40% of GDP in 1970. The current account was in perpetual surplus after 1965, apart from the two oil shocks. The economy was continuously characterised by a structurally excessive savings rate while policymakers failed to implement the necessary changes to lower it. The palliative in the 1970s and 1980s was cyclical reflation that resulted in gigantic house price and equity bubbles. Japan's development has been hampered for the two decades since they burst.

In China's first stage of development the savings rate gradually increased to a high of 42% of income in 1994. It then went down until China's entry into the World Trade Organisation in 2001, when it shot up by 16 percentage points in eight years. China's recession in 1994 marked a turning point for the economy. The currency was devalued by 45% and pegged to the dollar thereafter. Before that point China's high savings were benign. The national savings rate was high, but so was domestic investment, which often ran ahead of domestic savings to produce balance of payments deficits.

Between 1994 and 2000 China's savings rate declined, but the investment rate fell at a faster clip to produce a larger payments surplus than in the past. People saved less when the real return on their assets, mostly bank deposits, rose sharply. (It had fallen deep into negative territory during the high inflation period of 1993–95.) After the Asian financial crisis, the authorities' monetary stimulus boosted investment, lowering the balance of payments surplus, although it never quite moved into deficit. It was WTO entry that marked China's decisive move into excess savings, with the current account surplus reaching 10% of GDP in 2007 (Figure 9).

Both China's investment and savings rate have hit higher peaks than Japan's, but importantly the excess of its domestic savings over domestic investment has also reached a much higher level than Japan's ever did. The global impact of China exporting its excess savings and excess production, while devouring raw materials, has already been much more profound. At its 10% of GDP peak in 2007, China's current account surplus was way higher than Japan's 4.2% peak in 1986 or 2.5% in 1971. China's impact on the US (with the yuan–dollar pegged) and on the rest

Figure 9    **China's current account**
            *% of GDP*

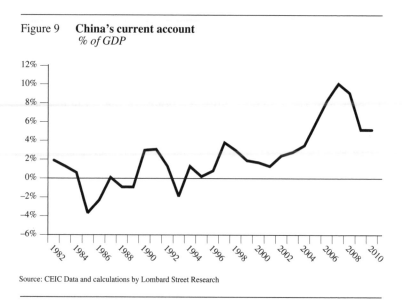

Source: CEIC Data and calculations by Lombard Street Research

of the world was bigger than Japan's impact during the Bretton Woods fixed exchange rate system. China's current account surplus was 2.6% of US output in 2007, compared with Japan's current account surplus of 0.7% of US output in 1971.

China's high savings provided the finance for the economy to industrialise fast (Figure 10). The investment share in output rose to 48.6% in 2010 from 35.3% in 2000. But the flipside is the low share of consumer spending. In fact, the consumer share has declined consistently since the start of the last decade, to just 33.8% of GDP in 2010. Consumption has grown fairly rapidly, but it has lagged far behind national income growth. China's high and rising savings rate hobbles the emergence of a mass consumer market. In the same way that foreign direct investment kick-started China's private sector development, trade integration with the rest of the world, thanks to WTO

Figure 10   **China's consumer spending and investment**
            *% of GDP*

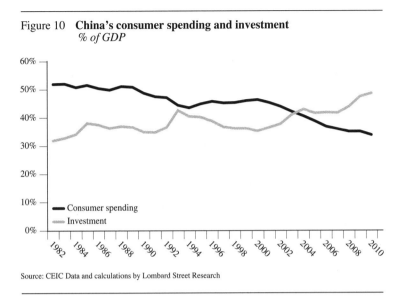

Source: CEIC Data and calculations by Lombard Street Research

membership, crucially provided foreign markets for China's surplus products.

## The usual limits to investment haven't applied to China

There are limits to investment. We produce more to consume more and we invest more to produce more. Producing more to invest more, when there is no increase in the propensity to consume or to export is a dead end. Producers need markets for the additional output which investment makes possible. But the more people save, the smaller those markets, making such investment unprofitable. Limits to social infrastructure spending are different from those that constrain business investment. Infrastructure spending is financed by taxation or government borrowing. But people object to paying high taxes, particularly where the tax system is inefficient or unfair. Borrowing builds up public debts on which interest has to be paid. These debts grow exponentially, if interest rate charges get so high that the government has to borrow to pay them.

However, the usual limits have hitherto not applied to China. China's investment rate is exorbitant. China's growth rate has averaged 10% over the past thirty years. Let's assume that GDP is 100. Then investment in 2010 was equivalent to 48.6. Let's then assume that GDP (output = income) continues to grow at 10% a year. It will then increase by 10 in 2011. In a developed economy, around one third of increased income goes into increased company profit. Two thirds goes in employee compensation to labour. But in China companies have claimed a much larger share of income as discussed earlier. So let's assume 6-out-of-10 goes to profit and 4 to labour. The gross return on capital is 6 (the extra income share) divided by 48.6 (the capital investment), which equals 12.3%. But China has invested too much in the past. Consequently depreciation charges are high, running at 7%. The net return on capital is 12.3% minus 7%, or about 5.3%. This is a seriously inadequate return on capital.

Profit is not the driving force in China's industrial sector, whether private or state-owned. In capitalist economies companies primarily exist for the benefit of their owners, the shareholders (in theory, although not always in practice due to the 'agency problem'). In China shareholders, whether foreign or domestic, matter very little. In the private sector, entrepreneurial managers are focused entirely on the short term. Chinese firms often rush to exploit short-term business opportunities, such as a shortage of any kind. Herd behaviour results in the quick build-up of oversupply. (A command economy with central planning is supposed to prevent competitive expansion in pursuit of collectively unattainable increased market shares. A market economy, devoted to short-term growth rather than profit, suffers this flaw.) Overexpansion drives down profit margins. Chinese managers move on to the next opportunity, often branching out into totally unrelated businesses. Hence, China, unlike Japan and Korea, has never created international champions in any industry. On the contrary, domestic export firms seem to relinquish a high share of the profits to foreign firms with established brands and distribution networks.

Overinvestment by private companies is cultural. Paradoxically it is economic in the state sector. The big state-owned firms in the protected sectors, such as oil, petrochemicals, shipbuilding, aerospace, telecoms, and so on, are profitable as far as managers are concerned because they enjoy a raft of subsidies and/or a state-protected monopolistic position. Access to cheap credit is the most important benefit they enjoy. Often zombie companies are kept on life support. The system of rationing bank credit according to the government's directives does not sieve profitable firms from unproductive behemoths.

Profits in a capitalist system are a buffer that keeps hostile takeovers at bay. Firms are keen to pass on cost increases to consumers even if they lose market share. Chinese companies have large fixed costs, accumulated during years of overinvestment. The low share of labour income, a variable cost in China, reduces marginal costs per unit output relative to fixed costs. Low profits on large sales are preferable to fatter margins on smaller sales. In the short term, losses are less from selling below average costs but above marginal than from suspending production. Admittedly, this would be true in a capitalist model, but it would be doubtful companies across the board would have overinvested to the same extent in the first place.

Operating in this environment for years, China's industrial sector has optimised its finances and operations to depend crucially on maintaining and increasing its global market share. The fear of losing market share and the fear of the unknown explain the authorities' reluctance to liberalise China's exchange and interest rates or allow faster yuan appreciation and higher interest rates. It is striking that even after engineering the most spectacular domestic-demand driven growth revival in the face of a severe global downturn, China's current account surplus was only halved in 2009–10, and its 'real' trade balance (exports and imports measured by volume) revived rapidly from mid-2009 despite the fast domestic growth boosting imports heavily.

## The financial crisis changed the rules of the game

The financial crisis marks the end of China's miraculous growth. It represents a major external demand shock. It has resulted in a prolonged hostile international environment of poor growth and heightened economic and financial turbulence. This is set to slam the brakes on China's wasteful muscle-bound development. Environmental and social constraints created by growth-at-all-costs and financial constraints created by the indiscriminate use of China's state-owned banking sector as an ATM machine building up a large pile of bad loans are set progressively to become more acute as China's growth grinds lower.

As long as the nominal yuan–dollar rate remains sticky,

rebalancing in 'Chimerica' can come from US deflation, Chinese inflation, or a combination of both. America's 2010 monetary and fiscal policy easing put China's feet to the fire by exacerbating China's home-grown inflation. Following the global financial crisis, China went yet again for a massive monetary stimulus and investment binge to pull the economy out of recession. It did so in a step back from the transition to market from command economy. It did not greatly increase the official budget deficit or government debts. It used the shadow budget, commanding state banks to lend.

Beijing insistence on managing the yuan–dollar exchange rate has created the most unsuitable monetary union one can think of. An undeveloped, poor, still largely command economy has been coupled with an advanced rich market economy. The prosperity of the poor Chinese worker has been made dependent on income transfers to the rich American consumer. To deal with its huge inflation problem, China's policymakers will now have to hammer growth. Meanwhile, US reflation is unlikely. Instead, a 2012 hard landing is likely (see Chapter 2) as the US still needs to sort out its excess debt problems. If Beijing does not budge on the currency front, it is entirely possible that the US will impose a surcharge on China's imports. Such a policy move will have an even greater appeal in 2012, a US election year. Pretty much all that Democrats and Republicans agree on is to blame America's economic woes on the foreigner – in other words China. The situation today resembles US–Japan relations in the early 1970s when President Nixon applied a 10% import surcharge. That was followed by the yen rising as the Japanese in their panic dared not to peg.

Whichever path China takes, allowing a large nominal

exchange rate appreciation, becoming uncompetitive through excessive inflation, or risking increased protectionism (not just from the US but Europe as well), it will face progressively slower export volume and value growth. Financing investment binges will become harder, as will hiding banking excesses. Like Japan in the 1970s, the inevitable fall in the capital investment to GDP share will lead to slower growth.

## What is China's optimal capital stock?

The poor return (excluding depreciation) to companies on gross investment has already been discussed above. Here the argument is continued in terms of GDP shares, the return to the economy as a whole.

There is an optimal capital stock for an economy. The best capital stock data is found in nine decades of US numbers. Since 1929, the capital stock has averaged three years' GDP, ranging from as low as 2.3 to as high as 4.25. But 4.25 was the 1933 multiple during the Depression. Excluding depression years the peak was 3.4 times. But let us err on the high side and assume China's capital stock should equal three years' output. US depreciation averaged 4% of the capital stock each year, but Chinese industrial data suggests it is as high as 7% a year. Given past wasteful overinvestment, not all worn-out capital needs to be replaced. Let us assume the middle ground, a 5½% depreciation rate, so with the capital stock three times a year's GDP, annual depreciation equals 16.5% of GDP.

Estimating the required growth in the Chinese capital stock, (net investment) begins with the assumed stock to output ratio, stocks equal to three times a year's GDP. It then looks at the different kinds of capital stock and how the demand for them is likely to rise. About 40% of the capital stock is in industrial buildings, plant and equipment (1.2 times GDP). Some 30% is in residential dwellings, or 0.9 times GDP. The remaining 30% is infrastructure and social capital, again 0.9 times GDP. Each of these shares can be multiplied by growing demand to determine the GDP share that net investment needs to take. The net share is then grossed up by depreciation.

Employment growth in China has averaged 1% a year in the past 20 years, but urban employment growth has been higher at 3.2% a year given the continued migration of rural workers into industry. Employment growth of 3% a year requires a 3% a year increase in the industrial capital stock (1.2 times GDP) to equip new workers, meaning net investment of 3.6% of GDP. Household creation has grown by an average of 2% a year over the past 20 years. This adds 2% to dwellings or 1.8% of GDP net investment per year. Existing workers need more capital to increase productivity. Suppose this is 4% a year, so that capital per worker rises from 1.2 times GDP to about 1.25 times in year 1. This adds 4.8% of GDP to net investment needs. So far required net investment totals 10.2% of GDP. Add to this the 16.5% of GDP depreciation and gross investment needs to be 26.7% of GDP. Make a generous allowance for infrastructure and social investment and the maximum gross capital investment requirement is around 35% of GDP. It is hard to put it higher than this. But the current rate of gross investment is 48.6% of GDP.

If China's investment rate needs to fall by 13 percentage points over ten years, the hit to demand growth will be substantial. Eliminating wasteful investment, however, will limit the supply-side impact on potential growth. Let's assume that real growth goes down to the government's 7% five-year plan target and inflation is 4%, so nominal growth averages 11% a year, and that in 2020, the investment rate is 35%. This means that investment has to grow by about 7.5% a year in nominal terms, compared with the average rate of 17.5% over the past ten years. And that's without considering the knock-on effects on consumer incomes. It is this type of arithmetic that underlies the demand-side violence of the structural adjustment that lies ahead of China.

## Investment constraints to kick in

The optimal capital stock is proportional to the expected output level. The capital to output ratio tends to be stable over the long-run. The change in investment is a function of the change in the growth of demand and as a result is the most volatile component of growth. In other words, investment is based on expectations of the future. In the private sector of China's economy the export shock is likely to change long-term demand expectations. The desire and need for investment will be reassessed even if financing conditions are kept benign.

Expectations hardly play any role in the state-owned industrial sector or in investment in social infrastructure. Given the poor rate of return on capital, the cost and availability of financing for the investment expansion will become the primary constraint. The banking sector and China's closed capital account are the crux of the issue.

As explained above, the banking sector is long on liquidity even if it is insolvent. Even after making the most drastic assumptions, China's total debt is not particularly high. Lombard Street Research estimates it at 215% of GDP at most. Bank credit is around 150% of GDP. Bank loans are the bulk of household and business debt. If all bank loans turned 100% bad and the government took them on as a one-off increase in public sector debt, the debt level would still be manageable. China's central government gross debt is officially estimated at around 30% of GDP. Bailing out bank loans would boost this to 180% of GDP on the unrealistic assumption of 100% bank losses. Foreign exchange reserves are 50% of GDP. Gross debt includes the cost of these. Local government debt and business non-bank debt could add another 35% of GDP to overall debt. Subtracting foreign exchange reserves and adding non-bank debt still leaves the overall debt total at most at 165% of GDP. This compares favourably with debt levels in the over-indebted Club Med, Japan, UK and the US. In the US total debt (gross household debt, net non-financial sector debt and net government debt) was 195% of GDP in 2009. It was 329% of GDP in Ireland (see Chapter 5). Even on the drastic assumptions above, China's debt is manageable, that is assuming the economy maintains its previous average growth rate of 10% a year and banks start being governed by market principles, so they do not accumulate new bad loans rapidly.

But sustained 10% trend growth and a sharp decrease in future bad debts, when the banking system operates according to market principles, are mutually exclusive. On the other hand, policymakers have some scope left to use the domestic banking system indiscriminately to bankroll more future investment. But if they do so they could easily push the overall debt ratio to unsustainable levels with a few years. In this case China will also need to keep domestic savings at home. Capital outflows must remain under direct state control. Beijing's recent measures to broaden renminbi use could be an important first step towards eventual convertibility, but for now the authorities do not seem prepared to open up the capital account fully. They do, however, realise the need to broaden their sources of finance for future expansion. Issuance of public sector debt is set to become a much more important source of finance going forward, as the role of the banking sector as provider of limitless cheap finance is set to change whether the authorities like it or not.

## Labour and productivity constraints to kick in

The human factor will also become an obstacle to continued 10% growth. China has unusual demographics for an emerging economy because of the one-child policy. The United Nations projects that China's labour force will grow by 2.6% in the five years to 2015, but then fall by 0.2% in the next five years. Over the following 30 years, it will continue to contract and in 2050 will be 13% smaller than in 2020. Labour force growth is one determinant of an economy's long-run potential growth rate, together with capital accumulation and productivity growth. Even though in a low-income, low-productivity economy, the scope for higher productivity growth can be the overriding force, China's dire demographic projections are going to have far-reaching implications for the very long term.

Over the next five to ten years worsening labour force developments are going to represent a less important constraint to growth. On the face of it, China still has an unlimited supply of cheap labour, with half of its population still living in rural areas.

But the most important labour constraint over the next five to ten years is likely to come from the fact that China has reached the stage where the quality of the labour force has begun to matter more than the quantity. As discussed earlier, China's sheer size means that the economy has already become the global manufacturing base for low value-added manufacturing.

It is on the verge of exhausting the easy productivity gains from transferring low-skilled, cheap workers from agriculture to low value-added but higher productivity manufacturing. Depending on the dataset used, gross profit margins have fallen during the last decade and since the financial crisis. Currently, labour costs are likely to be rising faster than prices. Nominal wage inflation has accelerated since 2009, but it seems that the surge in unit labour costs has much to do with a fall in productivity growth, not just faster wage inflation. The authorities' response has been to try and move the low-cost manufacturing industry inland where labour costs are lower. The hope has also been that being closer to home will also alleviate the social stress of dislocating low-skilled, low-paid migrant workers. The government is expected to provide affordable housing, at least initially.

China's authorities want to have their cake and eat it, moving low value-added industry inland to preserve China's low-cost advantage on the global market and prevent losing market share to economies with cheaper labour costs. At the same time, the authorities have identified a few strategic industries which they will foster over the next five years, hoping to turn the richer coastal areas into high-tech hubs. While moving low value-added manufacturing inland will do little to improve productivity growth, moving up the value-added chain in manufacturing is the only way for China to remain on a catch-up growth path.

But developing a high-tech industry will face two key constraints. First, China will require skilled and well trained workers. Training rural workers to produce garments or to assemble parts is much easier than producing blue-collar workers capable of sophisticated tasks. Educating and training them cannot be achieved overnight. Secondly, in a much more hostile international environment, China will face much stronger opposition to grabbing market share from the high-tech manufacturers, the biggest being the US and Japan. Moreover, foreign firms have now burned their fingers when it comes to China's disregard for intellectual property rights.

## China needs to ignite consumer spending

The most viable route for China to move to a sustainable 5% growth path is to rebalance growth towards consumer spending. Here China's size is actually an advantage. If the economy manages to ignite consumer spending, it is big enough to provide the markets needed for its own production. The rise of the Chinese consumer will be welcomed by the rest of the world. But while consumer-driven growth is now enshrined as one of China's leaders' top priorities in their five year plan for 2011–15, it is a daunting task.

Two structural factors are set to provide support to rebalancing growth in this decade. The first is demographics. The share of the population above 65 years is set to increase dramatically in the next 40 years from 11.4% in 2010 to 38% in 2050, with the jump during this decade being quite pronounced. In theory, the aging population should help rebalance growth towards consumer spending. Pensioners consume but they do not produce.

The household savings rate comes down while the household consumption rate goes up. But pension incomes in China tend to be a fraction of what people earn while working. Even if we assume that pensioners spend all their pension income, they could end up spending less in absolute terms than the share of income they devoted to consumption while working. The phrase 'China will grow old before it grows rich' alludes to this constraint.

The second factor is the income distribution. Normally this tends to be bell-shaped, with people on very high incomes and those on very low incomes being smaller proportions of the total than people on middle incomes. In China the low income tail is fat or the distribution could be double-humped. But still, as average income increases, larger parts of the population pass through the important income milestones which allow them to be able to afford the consumer goods and services they were denied in the past. China is on the cusp of such change.

Policy remains crucial for these structural factors to kick in full force. Given the nature of China's excess savings, the key changes needed to boost consumer spending are to redistribute income from the corporate to the household sector, for household wealth to be boosted and for the government to pool its domestic savings for its investment rather than 'print the money'. Trying to disentangle the fundamental reason behind China's high household savings rate is hard. Clearly increased uncertainty in the past ten years has played a role, but high levels of uncertainty have been a feature of China's development for years. Improving the provision of social security, pension and medical cover (and there has been progress on these fronts) should with time reduce the household savings rate. But such reforms will take years to implement and get entrenched in people's beliefs.

The fastest way to lower the national savings rate is to lower business sector savings by redistributing income from companies to employees. The most efficient way of achieving this would be to open up the capital account and to allow the market to set both interest rates and exchange rates. Interest rate liberalisation and the removal of credit directives will help strike the right price in the intermediation of domestic savings and limit wasteful investment. Nominal exchange rate appreciation will bring a rise up the value-added chain without inciting foreign protectionist retaliation. It will boost the share of household income as China ceases to have a limitless pool of cheap labour as higher skills would be required. Liberalising the capital account could well actually result in private capital outflows pushing the yuan down and domestic interest rates up. But higher interest rates will also boost household income as two thirds of household financial assets are in interest-bearing deposits. Household wealth and its potential to expand will be supported by allowing people to invest their savings in search of the highest return.

Another crucial reform beneficial for consumer incomes concerns the agricultural sector. Nearly half of China's population lives in rural areas, but agriculture remains woefully unproductive despite its vital importance to China's development. State land ownership is the key impediment to higher agricultural productivity and incomes. Leasehold tenants are always frightened of the state taking land back (eg, for a steel plant) and in any case have only a limited incentive to raise productivity by economies of scale, such as combining farms, joining together for collective irrigation schemes, and so forth.

The reforms outlined above will require the Communist Party to release its control of the economy by allowing market forces to play a full role. Beijing has correctly identified that the next stage of development will have to involve rebalancing growth towards consumption and conserving China's battered environment. The problem is that policymakers continue to believe that the best way for China to achieve these goals is the top-down, state-directed approach. Opening up the capital account, liberalising interest and exchange rates, and private land ownership do not seem to be on the agenda. The central authorities plan to boost consumer incomes by lowering income taxes or by direct income transfers. They are raiding state firms for more dividends and raising minimum wages to help them redistribute income. They are moving low value-added industry inland to preserve China's low cost advantage. They are planning to build low-cost social housing to resolve the real estate conundrum. They are trying to improve energy efficiency by tying local government performance to energy efficiency targets rather than liberalising electricity prices, which are controlled by the government.

While these efforts may have a short-term impact, they are unlikely to change the fundamental incentives that drive economic behaviour. China needs to change its growth model, but it remains to be seen whether it will have the political will to do so. The conflict between policymakers cosseting exporters, state-owned enterprises and banks, and the need to allow free capital movement and to let the market determine exchange and interest rates, if truly independent consumers are to emerge, is going to intensify. China has managed to pull through a series of hard reforms successfully in the past. But the last remaining necessary transition of relaxing substantially the monopoly on economic power will have to involve a fundamental shift in the behaviour of the Communist Party. The hope is that Beijing will see the benefit of doing that fast, but the potential for a destabilising economic crisis cannot be ignored.

Under any scenario, growth much above 5% is unlikely. The declining share of consumption over the past decade means that real GDP growth averaging 10% a year has involved real consumption growth of only 7%. If that rate of consumption growth continues in a consumption-led future – a tall order, considering the issues analysed here – then GDP as 'follower' will be rising by less, as investment falls back. For example, 5% real GDP growth for ten years, with consumption at 7%, would not restore consumption to its share of the late-1990s. And China will be very fortunate if this halving of growth can occur as smoothly as such broad-brush numbers suggest. In reality, the slashing of the investment contribution to growth is likely to yield a very bumpy ride, whatever the future growth rate.

# 4

# China's red-hot economy to slump in 2011–12

The force of the global financial crisis took Beijing by surprise. China plunged into recession at the end of 2008. In their panic, the authorities engineered an unprecedented monetary and fiscal expansion. However, with China's potential growth rate likely to be already down from the 10% of the past, monetary and fiscal ease did more to accelerate inflation than to achieve a sustainable boost to growth. China staged a spectacular growth rebound in 2009 and 2010, driven by investment spending. But as the economy already suffered from substantial overcapacity when loans became plentiful and cheap, there was a rush to borrow to speculate on property. And within just a couple of quarters the economy overheated. Inflation accelerated on all fronts.

Policymakers were too slow in withdrawing the policy stimulus. Their unwillingness or inability to rein in China's seriously overheated economy on time meant that inflation could only have been curbed at the expense of a sharp growth downswing. By the end of 2010 Beijing had woken up to the inflation danger and started tightening policy aggressively. Monetary conditions deteriorated sharply as a result, profit margins were squeezed and industry faced substantial power shortages, all combining to bring about the necessary growth slowdown. Much slower domestic demand growth, reinforced by a weaker external environment in 2012 is set to test policymakers' resolve to rebalance their economy and push forward with the hard reforms outlined in the previous chapter.

If Beijing gets spooked and goes for monetary ease and muscle-bound development in 2012, it will do more to boost inflation again and create fresh asset price bubbles, this time possibly in the stock market. The further China goes down this route, the more it risks seriously damaging its long-term growth potential, much like Japan did in the 1970s and 1980s when it was spawning the massive real estate and equity bubbles that burst in 1990.

Moreover, China now grapples with the challenges Japan faced in the early 1970s, but its standard of living is much lower than Japan's was then. This could either make the Chinese people more determined to succeed or it could mean increased social unrest if the transition is mismanaged. When economic power was transferred across the Atlantic, Winston Churchill said, 'One can always trust the United States to do the right thing, once every possible alternative has been exhausted.' Hopefully, China will do the right thing. But it is running out of time to try out all the wrong alternatives.

## China engineers a spectacular monetary boost

China's authorities were no different from policymakers across the globe in pulling out all the stops in an attempt to prevent the financial crisis from pushing the global economy into depression. But China was much more successful at stimulating its economy

Figure 11 **China's increase in broad money**
        *% of GDP*

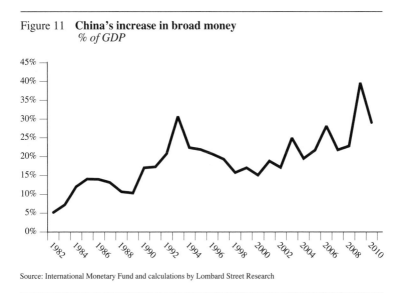

Source: International Monetary Fund and calculations by Lombard Street Research

and achieving a fast and sharp economic rebound than America and Europe. The immediacy and relentless force with which China's communist government could mobilise the mainly state-owned banking system to engineer a massive monetary expansion could not be matched in the West, where unconventional policies had to be pursued in order to bypass the blockage in the banking sector. China's monetary easing dwarfed the quantitative easing efforts in the rest of the world. But the monetary injection was also unprecedented for China itself. The increase in broad money was close to 40% of GDP in 2009 and 30% in 2010, compared with the previous high at 31% of GDP in 1993. To achieve the huge boost to money supply Beijing halted the ascent of the yuan, stopped sterilising the still massive foreign exchange inflows and ordered banks to lend (Figure 11).

China conducts monetary policy differently from developed

market economies because of its less developed financial system and Communist political system. China has had a fixed or a crawling peg to the US dollar since 1994. Monetary policy normally must be subordinated to controlling the chosen exchange rate. But protected by capital controls, China can have a semi-independent monetary policy. Export-led growth has been the antidote to excess savings since the mid-1990s. The pegged exchange rate and falling prices of manufactured goods have helped to generate current account surpluses. China's current account surplus thus reached a peak of 10% of GDP in 2007, despite policymakers allowing the yuan to appreciate by about 22% from mid-2005 to mid-2008. The current account surplus halved when global trade collapsed after the financial crisis hit, but it still remained high at 5.2% of GDP in 2009 and 2010 – and was only that low because import price inflation, notably of commodities that China uses profligately, had exceeded export prices gains.

To control the currency, the People's Bank of China (PBoC) is forced to intervene in the foreign exchange market to mop up the current-account surplus and capital inflows. It buys dollars and sells yuan. The relentless pressure of China's current account surpluses has been a tough test for the PBoC's ability to sterilise its foreign exchange intervention. But by and large the PBoC has succeeded by selling central bank bills and raising the reserve requirement ratio. Thanks to directing the four big state banks, China's authorities have control over the asset side of the banks' balance sheets This, together with capital controls, has helped the PBoC to pay interest rates below what it earns on its foreign exchange reserves, making sterilisation profitable.

In the middle of 2008, the PBoC halted the yuan's creep higher. It was thereby forced to intervene in the foreign exchange market on a massive scale. But this time around it had stopped sterilising its intervention, giving an instantaneous boost to money supply. The PBoC does not use policy rates to attempt to influence inter-bank interest rates and consequently retail interest rates. It targets the supply of money using an intermediate M2 target and an operational reserve money target. It sets retail rates directly by keeping a ceiling on deposit rates and a floor under lending rates to ensure banks maintain margins. Importantly, most, if not all, policy changes by the PBoC, but in particular changes to interest rates, have to be validated by the State Council. The PBoC is not a free agent.

Monetary policy in China does not have to 'push on a string', a problem central banks across the world have grappled with over the past few years. The phrase 'pushing on a string' refers to two aspects of the conduct of monetary policy. The first is that central banks may fail to expand the money supply. In a market economy they can set policy rates, but these do not necessarily filter through to affect monetary growth. The transmission of monetary policy can fail if the domestic banking system is impaired, whether it is through a hit to its capital or funding problems. At the end of the day, the central bank can provide liquidity to banks, but it is banks who decide whether to extend loans or not. Alternatively, it could be that the demand for credit peters out because of a previous borrowing binge. Central banks can also find it hard to battle against external influences, which could cause domestic yields to change dramatically.

The second aspect of the phrase 'pushing on a string' is used to describe a situation in which an increased money supply fails to push up domestic demand. The Great Depression and Japan's stagnation are often given as an example of that. But, these two episodes are in fact an example of the first aspect of 'pushing on a string'. Unorthodox monetary policy measures such as, put simply without going into the intricacies of open market operations and debt management policy, 'printing money' could have been used promptly and on a very large scale. The money supply has to be increased by more than the household and corporate demand for holding money has risen. It is possible to circumvent the zero interest rate constraint. But this was not American experience of the 1930s or Japanese in the 1990s. These examples do not prove that monetary policy can be ineffective in boosting domestic demand. Admittedly, if there is a complete breakdown in the production side of the economy, as was the case during the collapse of the Soviet Union and the Eastern Bloc, 'printing money' can fail, as it directly translates into higher inflation without boosting real activity.

China does not have the 'pushing on a string' problem used in the first sense. When Beijing tells banks to lend, they oblige, regardless of profitability, risk or reserves. The top management positions at the big banks are political appointments. Bank chiefs are not necessarily judged by how well they have managed their banks, but by how well they toe the party line. So there is very little resistance at the top of banks when it comes to directives from the State Council. When banks were given expansionary directives at the end of 2008 and deposit and lending rates were slashed, they obeyed, so credit growth exploded.

But banks will also embrace any market opportunity to make money if there is no specific government ban. Just as China's authorities were boasting that they had avoided the pitfalls of the Anglo-Saxon banking model and, consequently, a domestic financial crisis, Chinese banks actually started to engage in substantial securitisation in 2010. They were pooling loans together, normally high-quality short-term corporate loans, into wealth management products. These were sold at higher yields, transferred into trust companies and thus removed from the banks' balance sheets.

The surge in securitisation was a response to the economic and financial environment that emerged by the end of 2009. The huge monetary boost led to a spectacular and immediate real GDP recovery, but in the middle of 2009 the economy broke the 'speed limit' and inflation started to accelerate on all fronts. Consumer prices, property prices and wages all started to pick up speed. By the end of 2009 China's authorities were aware of the inflation problems caused by excessive bank balance sheet expansion. They started to put some pressure on banks to curtail lending and warned about tightening bank capital requirements, but they continued to keep interest rates unchanged at low levels. Accelerating inflation and stable nominal deposit rates caused real deposit rates to turn negative at the start of 2010. It was harder initially to stop banks from lending than it had been to start them.

Securitisation allowed banks to extend loans, circumventing existing quotas, and make money, but keep their capital to asset ratios at the required level and satisfy the regulators. A report produced by Fitch on the dangers of ongoing securitisation in the summer of 2010 brought the issue to the attention of investors. Lombard Street Research has done its own top-down estimates, which suggest that in 2010 loans equivalent to almost 10% of GDP were put off balance sheet. This means broad money growth last year could have been equivalent to 40% of GDP rather than the reported 30%.

## China overheats fast

To say that the Chinese economy broke the 'speed limit' in mid-2009 is shorthand for it overheating, meaning the level of output rose above the economy's potential. Potential output is not the maximum that could physically be produced. It is where spare capacity falls below the level at which inflation is steady. The closer an economy approaches the full use of its limited resources, the more prices rise to pull unused resources into production.

There was ample spare capacity in the economy in late 2008 and early 2009, because external demand slumped in the 'Great Recession'. Lombard Street Research estimates that China suffered a technically defined recession – two back-to-back quarters in which real GDP falls. The actual output fell well below its potential level, and annual inflation slowed quickly, turning negative in early 2009. The rebound was so dramatic that by the middle of 2009 spare capacity was largely used up. There were then too many yuan chasing too few goods and services. By the fall of 2009 the level of actual output was well above potential. Consequently, inflation took off.

How serious was the problem? Published data shows that consumer price inflation rose from a trough of minus 1.8% in the 12 months to July 2009 to plus 5.3% in the 12 months to April 2011. But this official data is likely to understate true inflation. China watchers have long believed that not every statistic the Middle Kingdom throws out is accurate. For such a large economy and with such unreliable data, it is imperative for researchers and investors to collect as many pieces of information as possible. The more pieces that fit into the same picture, the likelier that the picture is the right one. Beijing shows the world its inflation by

Figure 12   **China's inflation**
*The consumer price index versus the GDP deflator,
four-quarter change*

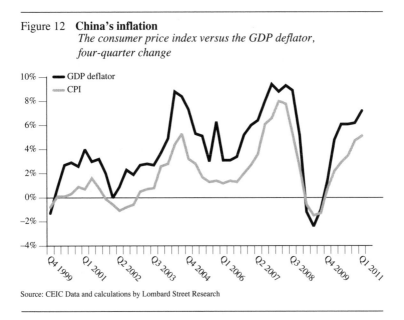

Source: CEIC Data and calculations by Lombard Street Research

releasing a consumer price index and most analysts focus entirely on this number. But if investors focus on the CPI as the sole gauge of inflationary pressures, they could underestimate the extent of China's overheating.

An important gauge of domestic inflationary pressures in an economy is the consumer spending deflator. It is an index of the prices used to convert current price consumption to volume or real consumer spending. It is weighted by the amounts people spend on each component of expenditure. The CPI, on the other hand, is based on a basket of goods and services whose weight is fixed for a period of a year or more. But consumers' preferences are hardly fixed for a period as long as a year: they tend to switch their preferences to the goods and services whose prices are rising at a slower rate. When prices are rising quickly, inflation measured by the CPI tends to be higher than that measured by the consumer spending deflator. The CPI will only reflect the switch in preferences when the National Bureau of Statistics (NBS) resets its weights (Figure 12).

China does not publish its consumer spending deflator. But the broader GDP deflator can be calculated from the difference between quarterly real and nominal GDP growth, both published by the NBS. This gives us the four-quarter rate of inflation for the whole economy. Figure 12 shows that the price level as measured by the GDP deflator has consistently outpaced CPI inflation. The GDP deflator captures changes in the price of investment goods, exports and imports as well as consumer prices. As such it is not entirely comparable to CPI inflation, but the comparison is nevertheless informative. In the first three months of 2010, for example, the deflator rose 7.2% from a year earlier, compared with 5.1% using the CPI. Of course GDP statistics in China are also inaccurate. Over the years real GDP growth has shown unnatural stability. But if the 7.2% inflation the GDP deflator calculates is an overestimation, this has to mean that real GDP growth was higher than the 9.7% Beijing officially clocked for that quarter. If real GDP growth was above trend in the first quarter of 2011 this strengthens the case for continued serious overheating.

Why the stark difference? First, while the market may set most prices in China, the authorities administer some – the key price of energy, for instance. And every time inflation becomes a problem, Beijing introduces price controls aimed at the items whose prices are rising the fastest. This happened in 2004, in 2008 and yet again in 2010 when, say, cooking oil came under controls. The CPI will take into account these administered prices – that is why it has not increased as much. The GDP deflator, however, includes the actual price of domestically produced energy, not just its controlled price to consumers, and it also reflects knock-on inflationary effects of imported price inflation. Secondly, the NBS changes the CPI weights only every five years, well behind structural changes in spending patterns. What's worse, the CPI weights are not disclosed, nor are the changes; some of the changes also seem to be ad hoc.

The NBS revealed that the composition of the CPI basket was changed in January 2011. It did not give details. The weight of food, hitherto believed to be around 34% of the index, was probably lowered and the weight of housing, believed to be around 14%, was probably increased. These changes could have been driven by genuine improvements, but the secrecy that accompanies them naturally creates the suspicion that the CPI is a 'politically correct' rigged index. Food inflation has been running at twice the rate of housing inflation.

The place where inflation would most naturally show itself is the place where demand is hottest. In recovery China that is investment and exports. Thus it comes as little surprise to find that in early 2011 the year-on-year gains in fixed-investment goods and construction was 6.5%, and for goods exports the inflation was more than 10%. Corporate goods prices were up close to 9%. Given the difference of 7.2% (compound basis) between the officially published nominal and real growth rates of 2011 first quarter GDP from the year before, it seems probable that the real number may have been closer to the truth than usual – ie, inflation was more than 2% higher than the 5.1% average for CPI inflation in the quarter.

But it is not just the prices of consumer (or other) goods and services that matter. Asset price inflation, most famously in real

Figure 13    **China's property price inflation**
             *12-month change*

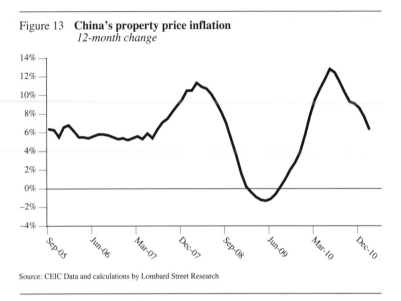

Source: CEIC Data and calculations by Lombard Street Research

estate, has accelerated, as has wage inflation (Figure 13). The rise in asset price inflation showed up the most in house price inflation, which went up to a high of 12.4% in the 12-months to May 2010 from being minus 1.3% to March 2009. The equity market has remained largely flat to slightly declining since summer 2009. But then the Chinese equity market experienced meagre real returns for years, followed by a large boom–bust. Hence, it was natural that investors shunned the equity market following the financial crisis.

China's residents started to own property only a decade ago. They have had very little experience with property market cycles and have not lived through a substantial bear market. Moreover, people who are not professional investors probably feel that investing in property is better as it is a tangible asset. In China only about a third of household financial assets are held either directly or through investment funds in financial securities, the rest held in bank deposits. The fund management industry's development has far to go before the household investment decisions are done predominantly by professionals. Consequently, it is not a surprise that excess household money holdings were funnelled predominantly into property. Other assets, such as antiques, furniture and gold, also saw prices spike up.

On the cost side, the labour market also perked up fairly quickly and decisively. Chinese economy-wide labour data is patchy, but both official data and anecdotal evidence point to a strong acceleration in wages. On the one hand, this was the result of the specific government policy of raising rural income. This, in turn, created labour shortages in the coastal areas, which saw migrant labour dwindle as workers preferred to stay in their villages. The real estate boom itself kept more rural workers at home. As cities expanded their boundaries further and further into rural areas, claiming agricultural land for real estate development, being a rural resident all of a sudden became quite valuable. The government generally compensated rural residents when taking away their land or buildings. Not being at home could mean that one lost out on this compensation.

On the other hand, the increase in wage inflation was the consequence of the general overheating in the economy. Local governments had to keep raising the minimum wage in a number of municipalities in 2010 and into 2011. Throughout 2010 there were an increasing number of labour disputes in private firms that led to substantial wage increases. Foxconn and Honda Motor Co were the most high profile. But from a structural perspective, the new minimum wage law issued in 2004 and the much-touted 2007 Labour Contract Law have enhanced the statutory rights of employees and impose greater obligations on employers. The authorities were also much more tolerant of extensive media coverage of strikes at private firms, in particular foreign-owned companies. But it remains unclear whether this new approach will apply to state firms.

## Beijing too slow to respond to the overheating

Chinese policymakers largely sat on their hands for a year and a half after inflation started to accelerate and a year after real deposit rates plunged into negative territory. They were woefully behind the curve, allowing a large monetary overhang to be created. So not only did the authorities increase the supply of money well above what was necessary for real GDP to grow at trend, but also because they did little to start withdrawing the stimulus on time and real interest rates turned negative, the demand for holding money fell as well. This Great Wall of Money was largely contained within China because of the closed capital account. The economy could not get rid of the excess. When individuals reduce their money holdings by buying goods, services or assets, the money just gets passed on to others. The system as a whole only gets rid of the excess money when prices go up to balance the demand and supply of money.

Why didn't Beijing start tightening sooner? Initially it was complacency. Chinese policymakers felt very good about themselves. They managed to get their economy going after a major external crisis, while the West was still struggling, even though pulling out all the stops. But it was not only complacency; Chinese policymakers also got newfound confidence in their top-down state control economic model. In easing, the authorities had retreated back towards the command economy. So in tightening, they did so in the same command way. They saw the biggest excesses in the housing sector, so they tackled it with administrative measures. But this was like squeezing a balloon: the air (excess money) just pops up in another place. Moreover, they tried to curb mortgages by fiat. But a large chunk of housing demand was financed entirely out of savings.

In early 2010 policymakers started to sterilise their foreign exchange interventions. By May 2011 they had raised banks' required reserves ratio three times by 150 basis points (again a command measure). But they were confronted with two things. First, they realised that sterilising, with US rates now zero, was not as easy as it used to be. The authorities could no longer ensure easily that the return on their foreign exchange reserves was greater than the rates the PBoC paid on the bills it sold to the banks.

But more importantly, the authorities were not confident that the global recovery was sustainable and their fears were confirmed when the European debt crisis kicked off in the spring of 2010. When that happened they stopped their tightening. In 2010 as a whole the authorities actually injected money in the interbank market rather than withdrawing it. The PBoC conducted open market operations to the tune of 683 billion yuan. This market move was offset, by the increased reserves ratio, which reduced overall liquidity later in 2010.

There was also another fundamental reason why they were slow. They had decided that they were comfortable with a higher inflation rate than before. Whereas the official consumer price inflation target in 2010 was 3%, the authorities gave the impression that they would be comfortable with 5%. The economy needed to rebalance, but a fast nominal exchange rate appreciation was considered a worse route. Wage inflation was welcome as it helped boost consumer spending and would not necessarily make exports uncompetitive. Policymakers failed to realise that wage inflation was an expression of generalised inflationary pressures and it was not clear there was much higher real wage inflation; certainly, not on an economy-wide basis. On the contrary, it is likely that China was in the midst of a wage-price spiral. The change in the authorities' perception came when popular discontent at the substantial rise in the cost of living started to rise. As the Communist Party's mouthpiece *China Daily* put it, people were unhappy with their 'inflation-hardened life'. The income and wealth gap between rich and poor expanded fast, and social tension mounted.

By the middle of 2010, pulling hundreds of policy levers at the same time had unintentional consequences. It piled cost–push pressure on top of demand–pull inflation. Chinese policymakers have multiple objectives and multiple policy tools. In an economy in transition, the command pursuit of objectives can result in counterproductive market responses. At the start of 2010 Beijing realised that it would fall significantly short of achieving the energy efficiency target set in its 2006–10 five-year plan. Word went out to local governments to intensify their conservation efforts during the remainder of the year. The central authorities made it clear that this objective would count in evaluating local governments' performance. The local authorities ordered a number of energy inefficient plants to close, notably in industries such as iron mining and steel production. As the year progressed and the targets were still not within reach, the local authorities adopted a blanket approach which saw energy supply restricted for industry as a whole.

Energy rationing, inventory rebalancing and property restrictions caused domestic demand growth to falter in the second and third quarter of 2010. But with export growth powering ahead, overall output growth was still at or above trend. Still China's domestic demand slump reverberated in Asia, causing Asian Tigers' industrial production and export growth to falter in the third quarter. Meanwhile, China's return to export-led growth saw its trade surplus expand, bringing down the wrath of the US again. Political pressure more than China's overheating pushed the authorities to relax the yuan–dollar peg in the middle of 2010, but the appreciation that was allowed was modest at 3.3% by the end of 2010. But by engineering power shortages the authorities reduced supply just as demand was booming, adding to cost pressures. This was visible the most in rising diesel prices. Companies fired up their own generators to evade electricity rationing.

The most important shift that finally compelled Beijing to start tightening aggressively came in the autumn of 2010. It was a change in American policy. US policymakers finally became proactive. Whether or not they understood it, they held the key to force China's hand. Keeping the yuan undervalued against the dollar deflates US demand. The US retaliated by reflating its economy with little risk of domestic inflation. Debasing its currency shifted the onus of the adjustment in Chimerica to China. It exacerbated Chinese inflation by curbing American deflation. The moment the second round of quantitative easing was trailed in Bernanke's Jackson Hole speech in late August 2010, global energy and food prices started going up fast. Imported cost–push pressures exacerbated China's domestic demand–pull inflation. (See Chapter 1 for a fuller discussion of this.)

## China's real estate boom is not a conventional bubble

After the Great Recession, everyone started seeing bubbles. After the US housing bubble, it was easy to transpose the same fears onto China when property prices rose fast and real estate investment picked up speed. The implicit threat of a bubble is that when it bursts the impact on the property market and the economy can be vicious. But China has neither the US debt-fuelled housing bubble problem, nor does it have Spain's decade-long output growth dependence on real estate overinvestment. While real estate investment played a crucial role in China's recovery, especially in 2010, it is important to understand the exact dynamics.

A bubble is underpinned by an excessive accumulation of debt vis-à-vis the ability to service the debt. The surge in Chinese demand for property in 2009–10 was driven by investment motives, which ultra-easy money helped spur. We estimate that 40% of the properties bought in 2009 and 50% of properties in 2010 were financed entirely from savings, not borrowed money. This, and the fact that mortgage debt is such a low share of income, makes it difficult to argue that China's housing market is a conventional credit-fuelled bubble. (Figure 14).

Financing home purchases with savings rather than with debt makes a big difference to how market excesses will unwind. When property is held without debt, investors simply have to contemplate opportunity cost, rather than face major negative cash-flow carry. Mortgage borrowing surged to 15.5% of GDP in

Figure 14  **China's mortgages as a share of GDP**

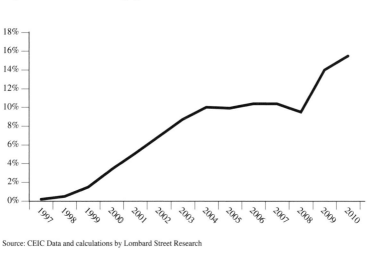

Source: CEIC Data and calculations by Lombard Street Research

2010 from 9.5% in 2008. Given banks' lax attitude to their loan expansion, enforced by the authorities, this was no surprise. But the increase in mortgage borrowing was only 15% of the total rise in credit in both 2009 and 2010. Between 2000 and 2006 the increase in US mortgage credit accounted for 46% of the total rise in credit each year. Overall, China's mortgage market remains underdeveloped when compared with the US, where mortgages equal 71% of GDP.

With a large chunk of house purchases financed from savings, house prices are less likely to be pushed down sharply by forced sales. Chinese people bought property for cash as an investment, expecting capital gains. They were not looking for a good rental yield. They are not paying interest to earn rent, they are earning rent instead of earning poor interest on their savings. In many cases they own unoccupied properties, willingly accepting a small regular loss from the (typically low) maintenance charges, in the expectation that the investment will yield an eventual capital gain. Hence, they are not forced to sell and will hold on to property rather than realise a loss. This is obviously a classic case of the 'greater fool' approach to investing – the assumption of being able to sell at some stage to a greater fool – but such bubbles can go a long way before falling back (or collapsing) 'under their own weight'.

Even those buyers who have financed their purchases with a mortgage are unlikely to end up being unable to afford the payments. The authorities have ramped up the down-payment for new mortgages and increased mortgage rates, but not too sharply for existing mortgages. Homeowners could be forced to default if an economic downturn leads to an increased unemployment. But they could default without necessarily incurring significant repercussions. The stigma attached to defaulting on a consumer loan that caused a number of Koreans to commit suicide when Korea's credit card bubble burst in 2003 is not to be found in China. Meanwhile, Chinese banks are unwilling to foreclose on delinquent loans. They don't want to realise losses, as they would have to put up more capital against them.

Real estate has played a disproportionate role on the supply side in this recovery. But China's overall growth has not been skewed entirely towards real estate investment for years, as was Spain's. Chinese construction accounted for 6.6% of GDP in 2010, up from 5.6% a decade earlier. In line with 5.8% in the US and well below the 12% Spanish peak during its construction frenzy. The government has stamped on what it terms speculative real estate development by restricting bank lending to real estate developers. This will hurt construction. By the middle of

2011 reports emerged that the big four state-owned banks had completely halted lending to developers. But at the same time the authorities have pledged to build affordable housing. The authorities have announced 10 million government-subsidised housing units in 2011 – though improvements to existing housing units are included in this number.

Despite the surge in real estate investment, China does not appear to suffer from substantial oversupply. The number of registered city households increased by 41 million between 2000 and 2009. There is no need to look before 1998 or even 2003 when the process of privatising government-built housing was finally completed. During the same period there were 37 million new units built. Data on floor space divided by the average flat size gives between 66 and 52 million new units (depending on whether you assume a flat's average size is 70 square meters or 90 square meters). The number could be even greater as residential space built by firms is not included. A PBoC survey, showing first-time buyers account for only 50–60% of mortgage borrowing, also makes a larger number plausible. But even were the supply of housing units one third greater than the number of households, this does necessarily point to a major mismatch. In 2009–10 the housing demand surge was investment not occupier demand.

The implication is that a housing market crash, resulting in an overall collapse of house prices is unlikely. House prices at the high end of the housing market could fall. The property market will remain thin until any cyclical excess is worked out. A thin market means that it will be difficult to establish a bottom for prices at the high end. In this case the result will be falling household tangible wealth. Households will be disappointed and will likely ramp up their savings, which will in turn hurt economic growth.

## Banks to bear the brunt of real estate excesses

Ultimately and most importantly, it will be the banks which bear any financial hit from China's housing excesses, as with China's overinvestment in general. The main hit to banks is unlikely to come from their mortgage lending, but their real estate lending. Lending to the real estate sector played a big role in the credit splurge. This is not necessarily visible if the official data is taken at face value. The increase in lending to real estate developers according to PBoC statistics accounted for just 5.9% and 6.5% of the increase in total lending in 2009 and 2010. The same data shows that housing lending, including mortgage loans, was just 15% of all loans in 2009. But the number is likely to understate the true proportion, as a big chunk of lending for property development has not been classified properly. In 2010 the PBoC itself published a study which indicated that loans to the real estate sector actually accounted for 40% of all loans in 2009.

A big chunk of the real estate development over the past year has been done by local governments through special financing vehicles. These vehicles are not classified as developers, although that is what they borrow for: to finance real estate development and other infrastructure projects. They pledge municipal land as collateral. Victor Shih, an economics professor at North-western University, estimated that as much as 12 trillion yuan, or 20% of all loans, have been channelled through these special financing vehicles. The PBoC and China's Banking and Regulatory

Commission (CBRC) have come up with their own estimates, ranging from 10 trillion yuan to 15 trillion.

Municipal governments cannot legally guarantee loans to special investment vehicles or indeed raise municipal finance by issuing bonds. But banks make loans in the belief that there is an implicit government guarantee. Local governments hope the land they pledged as collateral will go up in value when real estate or infrastructure projects are finalised. But the authorities became serious about restraining the increase in land values in 2011.

Newspaper reports at the end of May 2011 talked about the possibility of 2 to 3 trillion yuan of loans to the special financing vehicles turning bad. The government was reported to have plans to remove them from banks' balance sheets. It was not clear at the time of writing how this will be done. One option is to move them to the asset management companies (AMCs) that were set up last decade. On previous occasions when bad loans were moved to the AMCs, they were moved at face value. This time around maybe the authorities will make the banks bear some of the cost. But importantly, the AMCs were funded and continue to be funded partly by cash from the PBoC and partly by bonds that were sold to the banks themselves, while the PBoC took on the credit risk. The same creative financial engineering could be employed again this time around. But if it is, it may show as an improvement in banks' capital position, but it will still have a restrictive impact on banks' lending in the next couple of years at least.

## Beijing tightens too late, too much

The authorities, having woken up to the dangers of accelerating inflation in late 2010, are in danger of doing too much too late to counter it. Beijing has pulled out all the stops to rein in its seriously overheated economy. Monetary conditions have deteriorated rapidly so far in 2011.

The authorities have yet again used many policy levers. Between October 2010 and May 2011 they raised banks' required reserves ratio by 400 basis points to a record 21% for big lenders and 19% for smaller banks. It is interesting to note that while mopping up bank liquidity with one hand, the PBoC has been injecting liquidity with the other hand via open market operations. With US rates at zero and the yuan going up against the US dollar, sterilising the still huge foreign exchange interventions has become costlier because the PBoC cannot sell its bills at zero rates internally. It pays a much lower rate on banks' required reserves than on central bank bills. Hence it has preferred to mop up liquidity by hiking the required reserves ratio. On balance, bank liquidity has been withdrawn in an attempt to restrain banks' balance sheet expansion.

The authorities have also imposed bank lending restrictions more vigorously. Although they shied away from announcing a new loans target in 2011, they have nevertheless been putting severe pressure on banks to curtail their lending. The Chinese Banking and Regulatory Commission (CBRC), which was asleep at the wheel for most of 2010, woke up to the dangers of securitisation last summer. In August 2010 banks were banned from moving assets off balance sheet and told they had until the end of 2011 to return all outstanding amounts back on balance sheet. Banks began the process, but it coincided with liquidity being drained from the interbank market. Interbank rates shot up, halting the return of assets to balance sheets. Most of these products mature by the end of 2011. Hence banks thought they would leave it until the last minute to return what is left. Then the CBRC came out with a new directive requiring banks to return a quarter of all outstanding off-balance sheet assets every quarter in 2011. But despite the regulator's ban there are reports that banks continue to engage in securitisation and the CBRC itself is worried about the risks associated with 'shadow banking' activities.

The authorities signalled they were serious about tightening when, after the State Council's high-level annual meeting in October 2010, they raised both deposit and lending rates. By early July 2011 they had put up both rates five times, although the pace of increase was not as fast as during the 2007 economy's overheating. The authorities realised that there was a large monetary overhang and the demand for holding bank deposits had come down. So the best way to tighten policy, while helping the economy to rebalance from investment to consumption, was to raise interest rates. If monetary conditions were restrained entirely by administrative measures curtailing lending, the impact on the real economy would be much more severe because the monetary overhang would exist for longer.

Even so interest rates were not raised fast enough. Banking sector weakness was the main constraint, plus the economy's reliance on investment for growth. During the first three rate hikes the PBoC raised deposit rates by more than lending rates for longer than one year maturities. The authorities want to have their cake and eat it, focusing the excesses and this economic adjustment in the banking sector where they feel they have control and can hide the financial strains. But trying to keep control by relying more on administrative fiat may turn out to be self-defeating. Accelerating inflation could undermine Beijing's control of the banks if domestic savings start to flow out of the banks and into the black market or out of China through the somewhat porous capital controls. Playing with inflation is dangerous, not just because of the potential to incite social unrest but also because if left unchecked it can start to undermine the liquidity of the banking sector.

Other measures included price controls. But these either divert supply to black markets or necessitate rationing. The result is suppressed inflation. Ultimately controls curb demand but create distortions and confusion in the economy. Vegetable prices were rising fast in 2010 so the authorities capped retail prices and encouraged farmers to grow more. By the spring of 2011 there were reports that a supply glut was collapsing wholesale prices of certain vegetables. But instead of markets lowering retail prices, controls held them up. So vegetables were left to rot, causing financial distress among the farmers that bet on selling their crops. This story is slightly more complicated. The glut potentially made vegetables cheaper. But this was offset by rising transport costs. Retailers could not sell vegetables for what they cost, as the more they sold the more money they lost. The distortions from one control are often tackled by imposing another. The authorities asked local governments to step up efforts to help farmers by buying up their surplus produce.

An even more significant distortion was caused by energy price control, but that will be discussed in more detail later. Despite significant distortions and sometimes counterproductive results, the authorities remain stubbornly in favour of price controls and applying moral suasion to induce retailers not to raise prices. The national Development of Reform Commission, China's main planning body, went as far as fining Unilever 2 million yuan (£187,000) after the consumer goods group warned rising raw material costs could force it to raise the price of detergent and soaps.

The exchange rate has also been used to curb inflationary pressures. Greater flexibility in the yuan–dollar rate was allowed in June 2010, but more as a response to political pressure from the US than to curb inflation. Between June 2010 and May 2011 the yuan was allowed to appreciate by 5% against the US dollar, far from the sharp 15–20% nominal adjustment needed to help Chimerica rebalance. But the Bank for International Settlements estimates that China's nominal *effective* exchange rate fell by 3.5% to April 2011, while the yuan's real effective exchange was down by 1.8%. Hence, in terms of China's overall economy adjustment there was no progress. But with oil and most raw materials priced off the US dollar, the yuan's nominal appreciation vis-à-vis the US dollar did help alleviate substantial external cost–push pressures. In the spring of 2011 the authorities finally started to view the exchange rate as a tool to curb inflation, making a number of high-profile comments to that effect. But even so, Beijing remains fundamentally against allowing a fast yuan rise, preferring to see annual gains of around 5%.

The authorities' tightening quickly began to have an effect. China's monetary conditions deteriorated from the start of 2011. Broad money is the best indicator of monetary conditions. M2 is the broadest measure China publishes. On a three-month annualised basis, a guide to recent trends, M2 growth slowed sharply in the first five months of the year. It fell to an average of 10.4% from 28.5% in October 2010. Similar downturns occurred during

China's domestic demand slump in mid-2004 and when the economy was in the throes of the Asian financial crisis in 1998.

The deterioration in China's monetary conditions is also shown by the ratio of the increase in broad money to GDP. On this measure, the tightening also looks dramatic. Taking seasonally adjusted data for M2 and nominal GDP, Lombard Street Research estimated that the broad money supply increased by the equivalent of just 14% of GDP in the first quarter of 2011, compared with 32% in the same quarter in 2010.

In April 2011 the PBoC started to publish data on what it terms 'total social financing' in an attempt to address some of the 'shadow banking' issues. It even suggested that in time this measure could substitute broad money in its importance for policy. The measure is a theoretical muddle. It includes net equity and corporate bond issuance and is not a valid indicator of monetary conditions. But it did contain detailed information that allowed Lombard Street Research to estimate an adjusted broad money number, accounting for the bulk of the 'shadow banking' activities. The measure supports the assessment that monetary conditions have tightened rapidly so far in 2011, with the corresponding number in the first quarter of 2011 at 23%, down from 46% a year earlier.

State firms, struggling to secure finance, have turned to borrowing offshore from Chinese banks in Hong Kong. But while this development has had a significant impact on Hong Kong, prompting the Hong Kong Monetary Authority to sound a warning signal in April 2011, the amounts are immaterial, with the increase in those loans in the first quarter of 2011 being no higher than 3% of China's GDP. Private firms have also been struggling to secure funds, with anecdotal reports suggesting lending rates have surged in the 'grey' market.

## GDP growth must fall below trend to curb inflation

China needs to see output growth slow well below trend to cool its overheated economy and to curb inflation. There are a few mechanisms pushing the economy into this cyclical downturn. First of all, by being behind the curve in tightening policy the authorities let inflation rise fast, likely cutting into real consumer incomes and hurting consumer confidence. Hence, it was not a surprise that while real GDP still grew above trend in the first quarter of 2011, the overall strength concealed much weaker consumer spending growth. Mopping up the excess liquidity, together with property market restrictions, is likely to cause property prices to stop rising if not fall, thus raising the household saving rate as discussed earlier and hurting consumer spending further.

The sharp tightening of monetary condition in the first few months of 2011, if maintained for most of 2011, will undermine growth by cutting finance for investment in the state sector. Over-investment already means that profit margins in China are thin. Thus rising input and labour costs, together with price controls, have hurt profit margins further, despite the ability of exporters to raise the dollar price of China's exports. As discussed in Chapter 1, Lombard Street Research estimates that China's unit labour costs rose by 10% in 2010. The cyclical hit to profits and profit margins will curb private firms' ability and desire to invest in the second half of 2011 and into 2012.

In addition, by May 2011 China's red hot economy was again struggling with power shortages. China Electricity Council is reported to be planning an increase in its estimate for power shortages at peak times during 2011 to 40 gW, which would be

Figure 15  **China's utilisation of power generating equipment**

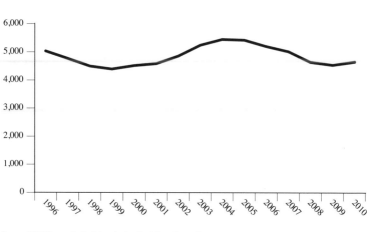

Source: CEIC Data and calculations by Lombard Street Research

as bad as during the 2004 blackouts. Anecdotal evidence abounds that power rationing was already underway in May. The problem this time around was not inadequate power capacity as it was in 2004. But in both cases power shortages have been the result of economy-wide overheating and Beijing's reluctance to allow the market to determine electricity prices (Figure 15).

In 2004 China was overheating after four years of rapid investment in manufacturing capacity, pushing the economy's investment rate to 44% of GDP from 36% in 2000. Overcapacity in manufacturing was quickly built up, but investment in energy and transport infrastructure lagged behind. The authorities administer the price of electricity, so while energy prices surged on global markets, China's manufacturers enjoyed cheap input costs which created a glut of manufactured goods, pushing their prices down.

But China could not escape the business cycle, so by the middle of 2004 the economy had hit its cyclical barriers. Massive power and transport shortages caused domestic demand growth to collapse, led by investment.

Fast-forward to 2011 and the story is similar. After the 2008 recession China's authorities flooded their economy with liquidity, fuelling rapid acceleration of domestic inflationary pressure. Over the past five years China has more than doubled its electricity-generating capacity, so this time around this was not the constraint. But Beijing's continued policy of using administrative measures has again played a key role. While the price of iron ore has shot up, electricity prices continue to be administered and have not kept pace, causing power generators to lose money. Power shortages are a powerful tool that generators can use to force Beijing to either raise electricity prices or dish out subsidies. The blackmail tactics were effective to an extent and the authorities did raise electricity prices in May for industrial, commercial and agricultural users, but not by enough. Moreover, higher electricity prices will either cut further into profit margins or get passed on to the consumer.

## Summing up: China faces turbulent years ahead

China's economy is like a gigantic pendulum. After the financial crisis the authorities pulled it violently in one direction. With the domestic economy overheated and the rest of the world poised for a growth relapse in 2012, the forces of the business cycle and sharp domestic policy tightening are swinging China's economy in the opposite direction equally strongly. For China's policymak-ers to achieve a balanced economic workout after pressing the panic button in 2008–09 has been a tall order. Another recession may not be on the cards, but output growth is set to be signifi-cantly below trend for most of 2011 and into early 2012. China's cycle has become shorter and more volatile, so the economy could rid itself of the cyclical overheating fairly fast.

The authorities then have a choice. Either stay firm in the face of adversity – a sharp economic downturn – or get spooked. In other words they can either continue on the path of reform to change China's growth model towards domestic consumption or they can revert to growth at all cost and go for another monetary stimulus and credit-fuelled investment binge in 2012. But if that is the path they take, it will work even less than in the last two years, as China has reached the end of the road for its purely catch-up growth model.

Here the analogy with Japan of the early 1970s is pertinent. My colleague Brian Reading wrote two decades ago, referring to Japan in the early 1970s: 'Like the cartoon character who walks over the edge of a cliff, but does not fall until he looks down, the Japanese growth machine continued to function in the minds of people long after it had no visible means of support.' The same is likely to characterise Chinese policymakers over the next few years. The authorities are talking about the need for growth to slow, but are they prepared to accept the social and political consequences of the change that lies ahead? The greatest problem they will have to contend with is coming to terms with much slower growth. Every time there is a cyclical downturn and policymakers try to achieve the growth rates of the past, easing monetary and fiscal policy will do more to accelerate inflation and create asset price bubbles than to result in a sustainable boost to growth.

Which way will the authorities go? It is difficult to say. The current political leadership largely wasted the good years by stalling reform. During the last decade there has been very little further liberalisation, in particular in the financial sector. But 2012 is a special year for China. In the autumn China's current leaders will retire and a new generation – the so called fifth generation – will take the helm. This is likely to mean two things. First, policymakers will be tough on the tightening front in 2011, but their resolve could easily waver in 2012, especially if the global environment deteriorates sharply. And, second, to be in a position to undertake painful reforms, the new leadership first has to establish itself and consolidate power.

In many ways this period is reminiscent of the early 1990s. At that time after a major monetary reflation the economy was also overheating. Inflation was high and growth slowed. The economy seemed to have exhausted the easy gains from the initial opening up, and major reform of the state-owned industrial sector was needed. Such reform seemed a daunting task and there were policy mistakes. But eventually the authorities got their act together and managed to get on with these hard reforms even though many observers at the time expressed scepticism. As discussed in Chapter 3, this time around to make the final transition, the authorities will have to release economic control considerably and fast. It is a tall order. Either way, what is clear is that even if China is ultimately successful at changing its growth model, over the next few years its growth is likely to be more inflationary, the danger of asset price bubbles followed by busts is high, the adjustment will be turbulent, involving financial distress, and the miraculous growth era of 10% growth rates is over. The 'China dream' many investors have will be tarnished, causing a rethink of global investment strategies and economic policy assumptions.

# 5

# Euroland's debt tragedy – Ireland, Club Med

The countries in EMU (Economic and Monetary Union) have lost their ability to manage their economies in much the same way, only more so, that the linkage of the US and China through Beijing's creation of Chimerica with its yuan–dollar peg has reduced the economic autonomy of the US and now China. Over the 12 years of Euroland's existence, Germany has, to no one's surprise, become excessively cost-competitive and therefore structurally undervalued, while Italy, Spain, Greece and Portugal – 'Club Med' – have become correspondingly uncompetitive in costs, and overvalued. In contrast to the US and China, however, neither side of the Euroland imbalance has had any growth of true competitiveness. True competitiveness is not achieved by cutting wages, but by higher productivity, output per hour worked. The combination of virtually incurable imbalances, major differences between countries in their economic priorities, and productivity growth that has been poor in Germany and France, negligible in Spain, and actually negative in Italy, is lethal. Euroland has condemned itself to a decade in which any growth at all will be a good result, and serious economic catastrophe is possible.

Ireland, interestingly, is one country where productivity growth has been impressive. Good results have also been achieved in Greece, as well as Finland within the surplus countries of north-central Europe. The relatively good performance of Ireland and Greece hints at the mistaken analysis arising from the common reference to Germany as 'competitive' and the crisis countries – Club Med and Ireland – as implicitly uncompetitive, with the further implication that this explains the current crisis. In reality, the distortions and imbalances that have arisen in Euroland reflect three factors:

1. differential rates of inflation, particularly labour-cost inflation, the chief divergence being not so much in productivity, ie, true competitiveness, as in wage and salary growth;
2. differential rates of growth, particularly repression of growth in Germany in 2002–05, which also contributed to its relative labour cost reduction, and (crucially) ensured a full economic cycle of low growth in 'Core Euroland' (Germany, France, Benelux and Austria); giving rise to
3. 'one size fits none' monetary policy, illustrated in Figure 16, with the vigorous growth in Ireland, Greece and Spain exaggerated and distorted (towards excessive construction and real estate) by interest rates too low for their needs, while in Core Euroland the vigorous fringe meant rates higher than were suitable given its sluggish growth, such higher rates further repressing demand.

The most tragic victim of all this is arguably Ireland, where growth was until 2007 excellent, both in productivity and employment. Labour costs never became significantly uncompetitive, inflation was moderate, and the government was running a surplus so that its 'net debt' was by end-2007 negative, ie, its financial

Figure 16 **Real short-term euro interest rates**
*1999–2007 average, %*

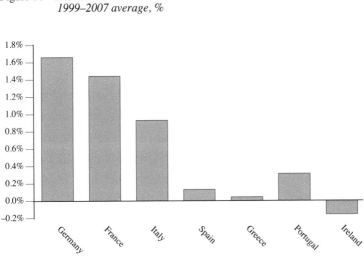

Source: Organisation for Economic Cooperation and Development

assets exceeded its (small) debt. Yet Ireland was the first of the five troubled Euroland fringe countries to hit problems. Membership of EMU has been a catastrophe. Since early-2007 the Irish economy has fallen 15% in real terms and 24% in nominal terms, the difference being a measure of price deflation.

The *laissez-faire* neglect of any serious bank regulation was clearly one cause of the huge swelling of bank loans, largely financed in wholesale markets rather than by retail deposits, that have brought Ireland to the brink of national default – a brink it is likely to tip over before the crisis is finished. But the chief blame must lie in the utterly unsuitable interest rates arising from EMU's 'one size fits all' monetary policy – in fact, as already stated, 'one size fits none'. These rates encouraged huge and excessive expansion of loan activity, goosing up a real estate boom that made such excesses self-feeding. The absence of any possibility of monetary restraint tailored to Ireland's needs meant that this crazy distortion of the economy and banking system towards construction and real estate continued until it collapsed 'under its own weight'. This collapse started before the subprime crisis arose in the US in mid-2007.

If Ireland (1.7% of Euroland GDP) was the extent of the problem, it would be simple enough for the system to bail it out, though the policy conditions attached would be destructively unreasonable and anti-growth. But various combinations of the three distortive EMU factors mentioned above have ensured that there is now a debt crisis in the whole of Club Med as well, so that it involves economies that comprise more than one third of Euroland, including Italy, or more than one sixth excluding Italy. Because the Irish problems surfaced first, the subsequent four years has given a clear illustration of how and why Euroland governance mechanisms are completely inadequate to deal with the problems that the euro has given rise to, and the disastrous consequences of the only available policy – outright and indiscriminate repression of growth – that demonstrate the grandiose folly that is EMU.

### Ireland's dire straits despite 'euro-compliance'

The chimera that the whole world can massively reduce government deficits by imposing fiscal deflation on already severely weakened economies took a further vicious step towards demonstrable failure with the end-2010 Irish bail-out. In 2007, Irish per head GDP was one third higher than the EMU average, and a fifth above the European Big 3 (Germany, Britain and France). Its government debt was offset by considerable assets: net government debt was nil (in fact slightly negative). Ireland had the debt capacity to deal with its overblown banking sector's major problems, and the income level to absorb a significant cut in incomes – to turn what was in any case good industrial cost competitiveness into a cost advantage that could stimulate economic recovery. As late as spring 2009, when the National Asset Management Agency (NAMA) scheme was first mooted, Ireland could just have emerged from the crisis with its economic model reasonably intact.

But the EMU structure is unforgiving. It leaves no room for error in the conduct of policy. And blunders there were a-plenty, as always when crises hit unprepared governments. The seriousness of the banking crisis was only gradually understood by the Irish government, which compromised its efforts to stem the downward rush of events by interpolating secondary goals – most importantly, its refusal to nationalise the banks overtly. The first advanced nation to guarantee explicitly all its banks' liabilities in early October, 2008, Ireland had by that action assumed responsibility for the banks. NAMA, rather than full nationalisation and work-out, was a classic assumption of 'responsibility without power', a lethal political trap.

The cost of Irish delay in tackling its banks' problems – once the option of letting some non-depositor creditors take some of the strain was let slip in late 2008 – was already clear from the 2010 budget deficit: 32.2% of GDP versus the already huge 14.4% of 2009 and 7.3% of 2008. Much of this deficit was to finance a one-off underpinning of the banks. But the other cost of delay lies in the worsening economy. Even at the level of real output, the Irish economy, though highly open and export-orientated,

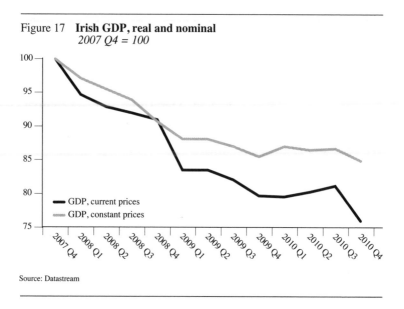

Figure 17   **Irish GDP, real and nominal**
            *2007 Q4 = 100*

Source: Datastream

continued to slide in the year from spring 2009, when the rest of the world was recovering – some of it briskly, such as the US and Germany, and in China's case very strongly. This was despite the fact that Irish exports had significantly outperformed those of other countries in the recession.

Ireland's loss of real GDP is bad enough – 15% in three years, far worse than other advanced countries' recessions. But Figure 17 shows how, by accepting the full, deflationary price of euro membership, the nominal economy – against which deficits and debts are measured, and from which they will have to be repaid – has done far worse. Nominal GDP is down by just under a quarter. This drop in nominal output and income means that any debt ratio is one third higher than it would have been in relation to 2007's income, so deficits have to be cut significantly merely to stop the deficit ratio getting worse – and an actual surplus is needed to stop the debt ratio getting worse. Leaving aside the one-off cost in 2010 of recapitalising the banks, the government deficit is in the 12%-of-GDP region, and the programme arrived at as part of autumn 2010's EU rescue package involves (on top of previous intended cuts) spending cuts of €10 billion (6% of GDP) and tax increases of €5 billion (3% of GDP). The total, 9% of GDP, together with previous plans, is supposed to bring the deficit down over 3–4 years to 3% of GDP, the Maastricht-treaty maximum.

This plan could well fail, at least once 2011's relatively strong world and European growth is followed by 2012's forecast relapse. Achieving the targets depends on significant growth of GDP, yet domestic demand is clearly hammered by the austerity measures themselves. So the hope is that Ireland's considerable cost-competitiveness will lead to a revival of exports (and perhaps a substitution for imports) that will significantly outweigh the massive net downswing of domestic demand. In its favour, it is in a much more favourable cost position than Italy and Spain. Also exports, at 100% of GDP, are much larger in relation to the total economy than in any Club Med economy. But a problem with this hope for the medium term is that slow growth next year in the US, and only moderate growth thereafter, combined with a weakened China, will knock on to Germany, whose exports are the chief possible growth source in the European economy: the rest of the continent is probably a lost cause. In Britain, importantly for Ireland, the domestic fiscal tightening and cost advantage from sterling falling against the euro will limit Ireland's potential benefit. So the projections of steadily and rapidly rising real and/ or nominal GDP look improbable. (Another major medium-term problem arises from the ignored issue of huge household debt, half as large again vis-à-vis GDP as those of the US in the sub-prime crisis, analysed below.)

If the nominal-GDP denominator continues to underperform, three things follow:

1. Most importantly, tax revenue will be below forecast, adding to the budget deficit.
2. The deficit will also be raised from its forecast as a percent of GDP if the latter shrinks or rises less than projected.
3. Rising debt in nominal euros, as the deficit continues large, will also be exacerbated as a percent of GDP by any shortfall in nominal GDP arising from price deflation.

This Irish trap follows from Ireland having pursued what might be called the 'Brussels (or maybe Berlin) prescription' for putting right the 11–12 year cumulative distortions caused by EMU mechanisms. In contrast to the IMF prescription – 'devalue and tighten your belts' – which makes eminent sense, the Brussels prescription is to avoid devaluation by tightening your belt much harder, to achieve not only deficit reduction, but labour cost cuts on a sufficient scale to restore competitiveness. The Irish example suggests that the Brussels prescription is likely to fail, even starting from a base of high incomes, strong productivity, which has kept costs competitive in the 2005–07 period, and low government debt.

Sadly, even if Ireland does achieve its growth and deficit-reduction targets, it still may have to default. In the analysis of debt presented later in this chapter, we see that household debt is half as great again relative to income as it was in the US at the peak of the subprime crisis in late-2007 and early-2008. This debt is only tolerable because the average rate being charged on mortgages is about 3%, as the Irish banking system is supported by access to European Central Bank (ECB) liquidity – at a time when the Irish government is paying more than 10% for its loans. This obviously absurd and massive inversion of the credit relationship between ordinary citizens and their government represents a huge subsidy from other Euroland savers (not just in Germany, but in Ireland itself) via the ECB. Once the rates on these mortgages rise to levels reflecting the country's credit rating, a large number of household mortgages will probably default. As the later analysis also shows, Irish companies' debt may also still be a latent source of fresh defaults, though in that sector the dangers have largely been brought under the government's wing in the National Asset Management Agency (NAMA).

## Club Med in a weaker position than Ireland

When it comes to Club Med, the starting point is far worse than Ireland's. Spain is the most similar to Ireland, Italy not at all. The similarity of Spain to Ireland lies in low debt at the start of the crisis in 2007 (net debt in 2007 under 20% of GDP, based on budget surpluses in the boom years) and fast previous growth. But Spain had an even more distorted emphasis on real estate and construction in its boom, as well as relatively low income and negligible productivity growth. As Figure 18 shows, Italy was in sharp contrast to this, with no growth at all over the entire recent economic cycle (measuring from 2001 trough to 2009 trough) and productivity that, alarmingly, was actually falling. No major economy has done anywhere near this badly since the Second

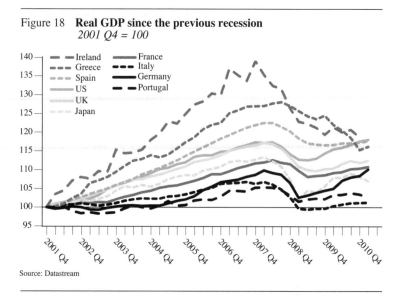

Figure 18 **Real GDP since the previous recession**
*2001 Q4 = 100*

Source: Datastream

World War. Italy's net government debt was very high to start with (on EMU entry) and remains over 100% of GDP. Its per-head income, reflecting poor growth, was also weak, by 2007 no higher than Spain's, which had caught up in spite of its own feeble productivity growth – Spain's GDP growth reflecting extra employment. Greece was like Spain in having fast growth, like Ireland in its good productivity growth, but like Italy in a high starting level of government debt that has been fed since with significant deficits in the good years, and large deficits since the crisis. (Interestingly, Greece and Italy, the two countries with a major government debt problem, have the two lowest total debt ratios of the five countries, once private-sector debt is included.) Lastly, Portugal, too, had very poor growth, mountainous private debt and by far the lowest income of the five threatened countries (and of Western Europe as a whole).

Figure 19 **Relative unit labour costs in manufacturing**
*1998 Q4 = 100*

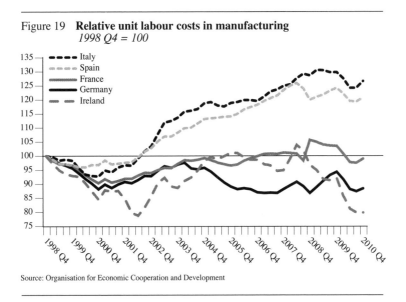

Source: Organisation for Economic Cooperation and Development

Where Spain joins Italy in the 'sin bin' is in excessive labour costs, illustrated in Figure 19. While the savage Irish deflation has at least cut its labour costs from about the Euroland average to a highly competitive level, Italy's are 25% out of line compared to the approximately 'right rate' at which it entered the euro at the end of 1998. Spain's are not as bad as this, as it came into the euro 10% or so 'cheap' in late-1998, but are probably some 10% overvalued now. These labour cost comparisons show costs per unit of output in manufacturing, measured against the weighted average of those of each countries' trading partners (including both the export and import side).

Greece's overall private-sector unit labour costs have also soared, though its chief problem was and is excessive government debts and deficits. As well as these weak public finances, Greece simply grew so much faster than core Europe that its finances were bound to get steadily out of line, requiring capital inflows, a characteristic it shared with Ireland and Spain. For each of these countries a major part of their problem has arisen from Germany's deliberate repression of domestic incomes and growth. Starting from a high national debt level, and never weaning itself off structural government deficits, Greece entered the crisis with a poor balance sheet and still-low income (despite some catch-up in the fast-growth years).

Without the European Financial Stability Facility (EFSF), launched in May 2010 in response to the Greek crisis, Greece would be in default already, as would Ireland and Portugal, and probably Spain too. Greek measures to slash the budget deficit have led to income collapse that is hitting tax revenue. So, in the footsteps of Ireland, Greece's programme to comply with its European 'partners' and attempt to avoid default is self-thwarting as well as violently self-destructive. From time to time, Greece will be coming back to Brussels (or Berlin) to admit that the targeted budget improvement cannot be achieved. Portugal and Spain are engaging in similar fatuous and self-defeating exercises in income destruction. Even in 2011, which is probably the last strong year for European growth for the indefinite future, these countries all have depressed and mostly falling output. When the harsher external conditions kick in, from 2012 onward, their prospects are dismal.

Italy's non-growth (like Japan's before it) could therefore be the model for the next decade in Club Med if it stays within EMU. Simply joining EMU seems to have combined with its hobbled supply side to prove enough to crush Italian growth. Its unemployment has remained quite low partly because much of it is disguised within family firms, partly because of weak population growth, but mostly because of actual cycle-long declines in productivity, reflected in falling real incomes: if output per worker is falling, output can fall without the number of jobs being cut, but incomes will decline instead. In Spain since 2007, where the initial shedding of casual labour has raised productivity (for the first time for a decade) and the economy was previously dynamic, with rising average incomes, medium-term relief to unemployment from falling productivity is unlikely to be available – nor should it be hoped for. Spanish unemployment, 8% in 2007, is now over 21%, implying that the true full decline in GDP is being concealed. (The mixture of bluff and denial in Spain's handling of its crisis emerges too with respect to bank solvency, see p. 150–51 below.)

In both Italy and Spain, the needed downward adjustment of wage costs relative to Germany, by at least a fifth for Italy and probably a tenth for Spain, is a chief reason why continued membership of EMU will probably ensure a decade of stagnation at best – possibly outright real income decline. It must be remembered that the grim recent examples of non-growth in debt-laden Japan and Italy occurred against the backdrop of a booming world, flush with credit. Conditions over the next several years are likely to be much tougher, fundamentally because Uncle Sam is no longer going to be bank-rolling the world in his past style.

It seems likely that, if the EMU governments persist in trying to sustain the ramshackle euro structure, severe deflation in Club Med, probably accompanied by defaults in Greece, Ireland, Portugal and Spain, will mean prolonged and major subsidy and credit support for those economies, largely funded by Germany. If so – and it cannot be avoided without expulsion of some members from the euro – German citizens could become deeply discontented with EMU and clamp down even harder than before on their own spending. In that case, the entire continent could enter Depression. Much is made of the US as a precedent for the formation of an economic union in Europe, but it is often forgotten that the US federal system was formed in response to the Depression.

## Debt by country – grand totals, not just government

To judge the threat of default by a country, it is necessary to look at the aggregate of government, household and non-financial business debt. The aim is to identify which countries, and sectors within those countries, need closer analysis to assess whether debt levels threaten government or banking solvency – or, less drastically, the ability to grow in line with the country's inherent productive capacity. For government debt, financial assets are netted against gross debt, as many governments have part of their debt offset by easily realisable assets. In general, net government debt is the better measure of potential jeopardy.

For business debt, it is also best to focus chiefly on *net* debt. This has dangers, as one company's strong cash position is not available to another with debts and no cash. And in any case, the cash position cannot be run down to zero. But we are concerned with a general, nationwide assessment of the sustainability of debt. There will always be individual companies going bust. The question is what are the desirable limits for the aggregates. As we have been through a decade in which the cash position of companies in most developed countries has improved significantly relative to measures such as gross operating cash flow (pre-depreciation, ie, earnings before interest, tax and depreciation or EBITDA) or pre-interest profit (EBIT) it would give rise to an unduly alarmist conclusion to ignore the cash that in many cases mitigates net debt. Nonetheless, it is desirable to keep a weather eye on gross debt. Business debt will normally be considered in its relation to operating profit after depreciation (EBIT) as depreciation represents the funding for replacement investment, which is needed if the country's capital stock is to be maintained.

For the total debt ratio of a nation, gross household debt is added to net government debt, together with net non-financial business debt. Devotees of gross debt ratios are right that in a crisis it is gross debt that matters. But the purpose of this chapter is to discover who is seriously vulnerable, ie, who is liable to be in crisis at some stage, not the likely precise course of events when crisis strikes. For this purpose the netting criteria for government and company debt seem appropriate. Results are in Table 2. As 2009 is the latest full year with available data for most countries, net government debt for end-2010 is included for reference. The US is included, as its excessive household debt caused the start of the subprime crisis in 2007, and thus represents a yardstick against which other countries' household debt can be measured. The UK is there for similar reasons as its household debt exceeds the US ratio, though it is put in the shade by Ireland's. Japan is in the table as a reference point for excessive government debt, and evidence of how it can be borne for a long while if growth is low and prices deflating.

Private-sector debt can morph into government debt when it exceeds the private sector's ability to pay, generally by means of a banking crisis: the banks' assets are the private non-financial

Table 2  **Key ratios of debt to GDP by country, 2009**

|  | Households, gross (%) | Non-financial companies, net (%) | Government, net (%) | Total (%) | Memo: net gov't 2010 (%) |
|---|---|---|---|---|---|
| US | 96.1 | 38.7 | 59.8 | 194.5 | 64.8 |
| Japan | 65.5 | 57.9 | 110.0 | 233.4 | 117.5 |
| UK | 103.5 | 72.4 | 60.9 | 236.9 | 69.4 |
| Germany | 63.4 | 47.7 | 55.9 | 167.0 | 53.8 |
| Ireland | 120.6 | 170.6 | 38.0 | 329.3 | 69.4 |
| Greece | 52.4 | 48.8 | 126.8 | 228.0 | 142.0 |
| Portugal | 96.8 | 137.6 | 71.9 | 306.3 | 79.1 |
| Spain | 86.0 | 115.5 | 41.8 | 243.3 | 48.8 |
| Italy | 42.2 | 65.6 | 97.1 | 204.8 | 99.6 |

sector's debts, so major debt service problems can render banks insolvent. This means Ireland and Portugal are at risk in terms of total debt, even though their 2010 net government debt levels were not especially high. Japan, Britain and Spain form a second group, with total debt around 240% of GDP, despite the considerable netting that has preceded calculation of these ratios. Of these three, Japan is the most feared as a source of future crisis, as its debt has largely 'migrated' to the government already. Its problems, and Britain's, will be analysed in Chapter 7. But current focus on EMU problems means Spain's grossly excessive company debt may cause problems in the relatively short term. In Greece, government debt is a huge problem, and to a lesser extent Italy, with a net government ratio of around 100%. The US, with almost Italy's ratio of total debt, could be in the same position in two to three years, with further private-sector deleverage and government deficits – but with, however, a much healthier potential growth rate.

Figure 20 **Household debt**
*% of gross household disposable income*

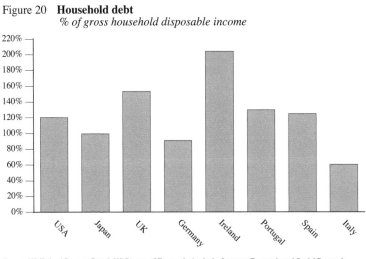

Source: US Federal Reserve Board, US Bureau of Economic Analysis, Japanese Economic and Social Research
Institute, and Eurostat

In the Irish data, a major jump between the end-2007 non-financial company (NFC) debt levels and those of end-2009 remains to be adequately explained. Nonetheless, the business sector bad debts to be funded by the government, both those taken over by the NAMA and others, are likely to be supplemented soon by household defaults, given the exceptionally high ratio of such debt to income. Apart from Ireland's banking system problems based on both household and company debt excesses, the countries where household debt is the chief problem are Britain, the US, also Portugal, and to a lesser degree Spain. This is best analysed in relation to personal disposable income. (Net wages and salaries are available for the UK, but international comparisons are not possible.) Company debt is the chief risk in Portugal and Spain, and their banking systems appear seriously vulnerable. In Greece and Italy the banking system is threatened by owning large slices of government debt, and depending on the 'credit of the country'.

## Household debt: Ireland, Portugal, Spain

Ireland's household debt to *gross* disposable income ratio in 2009 was 204%, far above even Britain's 153% let alone the US 121% (Figure 20). The Irish legal situation is much like Britain's, and unlike the US, where (crucially) mortgage-borrowers can in most states 'walk away' from servicing their loans by abandoning the house to the lender. In Europe, lenders generally have an unsecured charge on the borrower's income, as well as the house as collateral. Ireland is like Britain in 'national habit' too – ie, greater willingness than in the US to curtail normal goods and services purchases – and in the lesser importance than in America of extreme inequalities of income. But its former housing boom, resulting excess supply and house price crash are more like America than Britain, where planning and other bureaucratic obstacles held back the house-building response to the house price boom. Moreover, in the as yet unresolved euro-crisis, it is hard to see how Irish banks can avoid ultimately paying rates on their funding that corresponds to the now huge (over 10%) yields of Irish government bonds. Irish mortgages in mid-2011 cost some 3–3¼%, reflecting the same typically floating-rate structure as in Britain. But the borrowers are likely to be hit by major increases in interest burden over time, given Irish government bond yields stretching from 7% at a one-year maturity to around 11% for maturities of two years or more.

Right now, Irish mortgages are effectively subsidised by their banks' access to massive ECB funding, but even if this lasts it is highly unlikely to be offered for long at the same rate for Ireland as for core-euro countries such as Germany. So the Irish household debt load will probably provoke major further defaults, in debts that by now total over 200% of disposable income, 130% of a GDP denominator that is still declining. The early-2011 study of Irish banks, so-called stress tests, leading to yet another recapitalisation, did not take account of this likely increase in funding costs, and resulting household mortgage defaults. It follows that the bad news on Irish banks is not yet fully out in the open.

In Portugal and Spain, household debt ratios are significantly less than Britain's. On the interest rate front, the exposure is not so high for Spain. Portugal's government rates are downward sloping between two and ten year maturities in the same 10–11% region as Ireland's. The potential interest rates to be paid eventually on its mortgages is similar to Ireland's, though the total principal is significantly lower relative to GDP and disposable income. Its household debt ratio to GDP is similar to the US and below Britain's, though it worsens vis-à-vis both in relation to disposable income. As the funding rates for its banks move up over time, significant household default problems seem likely. Spain's interest rates are much lower, as well as its household debt ratio. They stretch from 3½% at short maturities to 5.6% at the ten-year, 3% above German Bunds. It is unlikely that Spain's government bond differential versus Bunds will stay this low, but the absolute rates in prospect, together with the less extreme debt ratios, argue for only modest Spanish default rates among households.

## NFC debt: Ireland, Portugal and Spain

Mergers and acquisitions (M&A) professionals treat debt of five times EBITDA (operating cash flow before depreciation) as the threshold of junk status. But for a whole economy – as opposed to a leveraged buy-out that may have under-exploited assets or other reasons for deferring replacement cap-ex – depreciation cash is needed to replace operating assets. So it is out of EBIT (operating profit after depreciation) that debt must be serviced, and the debt ratio to EBIT is therefore the most appropriate. Figure 21 shows that EBIT was typically about half EBITDA in 2009 – ie, the debt ratio to EBIT was about twice as large as that to EBITDA. In a strong recovery, the bulk of the extra business cash flow would go into EBIT rather than depreciation, helping this ratio decline. So a crucial question becomes how strong a recovery is likely and/or sustainable for countries whose company debt ratios are vulnerable. One exceptional case is Ireland, where very large, yet to be documented additions to company debt were registered by Eurostat between 2007 and 2009.

For an individual company, it might be considered acceptable for EBIT to cover interest by two times. But for a whole economy, especially with the debt being considered net of cash (which may not be available to firms that get into trouble) EBIT should cover interest at least three times. A net-debt/EBITDA ratio of 5 (the M&A junk threshold) implies 10 times EBIT, if depreciation is half EBITDA. With normal interest rates – as opposed to the emergency low rates now prevalent – firms could be paying net interest on net debt of 7%, more if considered highly leveraged. On debt of 10 times EBIT, the interest charge at 7% is 70% of EBIT, ie, only 1½ times covered by EBIT. This

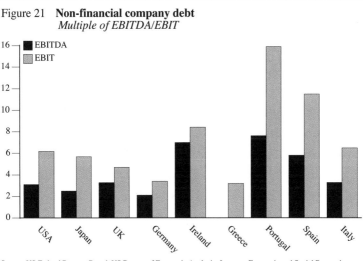

Figure 21 **Non-financial company debt**
*Multiple of EBITDA/EBIT*

Source: US Federal Reserve Board, US Bureau of Economic Analysis, Japanese Economic and Social Research Institute, and Eurostat

justifies the designation 'junk' (especially as the interest rate on junk is usually well above 7%).

For interest to be covered three times by EBIT, net debt of the NFC sector would have to be only 5 times EBIT(2½ times EBITDA) assuming a 7% interest rate. On this basis, Ireland, Portugal and Spain all appear to be in serious trouble with current NFC debt levels – especially as the zero growth of Italy over the past entire economic cycle could be replicated for the whole of Club Med, and maybe even Ireland if there is no debt relief. Even assuming weak growth, implying below-normal euro interest rates for the medium term, the current financial market attitude to these countries would make a 7% interest rate for NFC borrowers an extremely optimistic assumption, unless the credit support from 'core' Euroland is much stronger and clearly longer-lasting than has so far been indicated as acceptable, especially in Germany. In these countries, therefore, we are talking of the entire NFC sector being junk.

For the banks to be in much more serious trouble than has so far been acknowledged (except possibly in Ireland) only a portion of the companies have to hit the rocks. With Euroland hit by a variety of country crises over the past 18 months, the measures taken to 'tighten belts' ensure that growth is improbable over the medium term in Club Med, so that the business cash-flow position could get worse. Meanwhile, these companies are in many cases only solvent because the ECB is funding Club Med and Irish banks at what are clearly subsidised rates, given their evident likelihood of partial default. In other words, full-scale Core Euroland subsidy for Club Med and Ireland is already in force, and will have to continue – at huge expense to European savers – probably for the next decade at least – perhaps much longer, to judge by Japanese experience in dealing with similar problems. Needless to say, the Core Euroland grantors of such subsidies will be constantly on the look-out for ways to reduce this cost, so banks in countries at risk could be paying more for their funding over time, and charging more for loans to companies.

It is instructive to calculate the break-even interest rate at which interest on business debt would absorb all of the country's companies' EBIT – though this is clearly a situation that cannot be reached as major bankruptcies would pre-empt it. Thus, Portugal's net company debt at 16 times EBIT only has to be charged a 6½% rate to leave no pre-tax profit for the entire country's company sector. Portuguese business is clearly structurally bankrupt. For Spain, with debt at nearly 12 times EBIT, the interest rate to wipe out EBIT is about 8½%. While such a rate may not be reached on Spanish bank loans, it is clear that major bankruptcies are probable over the next few years, given the country's inability to grow, owing to uncompetitive labour costs and slow productivity growth over a long period. It only requires the weaker companies to be in debt difficulties to create a banking crisis, not the entire sector to have to pay away its entire operating profit in interest charges.

Ireland, with non-financial companies' net debt over 8 times their EBIT, has a breakeven interest rate of about 12% to wipe out EBIT. With Irish ten-year government bonds yielding over 10% this would not be an implausible number, except that the Eurostat debt data has two flaws: first, a huge jump in Irish NFC debt in 2008 and 2009 that is unexplained, and second, some of the worst of the company debt being already on the government's books under the NAMA arrangement. But the Irish company position is still vulnerable, though it looks less threatening than the household debt level.

## Government debt: Greece, Italy and Japan

While private-sector debt excesses are liable to morph into high government debt levels via banking crises, the debt problem has always been at government level in Greece and Italy. Of the two, Greece is an intractable problem – Italy has 'dealt with' the risks arising from excessive debt, and sustained uncompetitive labour costs, by effectively abandoning growth: Italy's real GDP is less than 1% above its level at the end of the previous recession in 2001. Greece came into the euro late, in 2001, with a high level of government debt, and achieved rapid growth until 2007 with continued large annual government budget deficits. Its end-2010 net government debt was 142% of GDP, and its government bonds yield over 20% at two- to four-year maturities reaching down to 16% at ten years. Debt service to some extent is held down by the lower cost of bonds issued in better days, but interest charges on the budget had already reached 6.4% of GDP by 2010. Given the debt level and bond yield, it is hard to believe they will not move up to more than 10% of GDP soon – unless comprehensive and long-lasting Euroland subsidies for vulnerable Club Med countries are established.

If/when Greek government interest payments exceed 10% of GDP, restraint of the government deficit to 3% of GDP – the medium-term target, and Maastricht limit, that is also essential to stabilise the debt ratio rather than seeing it mount indefinitely – will require a 'primary' budget balance of 7% surplus or more. The primary balance was *minus* 10% in the disaster year 2009, and improved to minus 4–5% in 2010 (gradually being revised for the worse). But progress from there to plus 7% hardly looks possible as the drastic budgetary deflation undertaken to make 2010's progress has sent the economy into a dangerous tail-spin. Aside from cutting the denominator (GDP) of the debt and deficit ratios – making them automatically worse – this loss of income directly threatens tax revenue shrinkage, thwarting efforts to cut the deficit. In other words, Greece is now well down the path trodden by Ireland, but in a country with a much more acute labour cost and high-interest-rate problem, as well as a much smaller export sector to offset domestic deflation.

In addition to the economic and financial realities, political commitment to the drastic austerity needed to achieve the budget turnaround is weakening rapidly as the pain intensifies, unemployment mounts and income losses become widespread.

Unemployment, 7% at end-2008, had more than doubled to 16% by spring 2011. But even with a fully committed body politic, the crucial point is that the mathematics of budgetary transformation to primary surplus are not feasible in the context of a European economy whose overall growth prospects are minimal after 2011's German-export-led growth. Greece has neither Ireland's low relative labour costs nor its large relative export markets to hold up income and therefore tax revenue. (Exports in Ireland are 100% of GDP, but in Greece only 20%, a very low ratio for a small economy.) The government debt ratio to GDP therefore seems likely to mount indefinitely. This means default.

Italy is clearly less badly placed than Greece. Its net debt ratio is 100% of GDP and its government deficit in 2010 was 4½%. But to stabilise debt at 100% of GDP, the deficit must not exceed the nominal growth of GDP. Over the past economic cycle, despite virtually nil growth, moderate inflation has keep nominal growth positive, so the GDP denominator of all these ratios has grown somewhat. But in future, with Italy's labour costs seriously excessive and no greater likelihood of real growth than in the recent past, domestically generated inflation could come down to very low rates, with deflation entirely possible. The future growth rate of nominal GDP could be minimal, or even negative. This means that to stabilise the debt ratio at or near current levels, the government deficit must be cut virtually to nil, and certainly well below the 3% Maastricht limit. This is unlikely to happen, so Italy's government debt ratio is likely to carry on up, if only relatively slowly.

Before Italy reaches crisis, however, the more dangerous situations of Greece, Ireland, Portugal and Spain (the latter three in the private sector, rather than government debt) are likely to have

forced action by European governments in a much more comprehensive fashion than the 'fire-fighting' that has been the response
so far to the debt and deficit problems of the peripheral countries. Any such broader approach to the debt issues will determine whether Italy moves forward to centre-stage and becomes
an immediate problem, or has a context within which it can work
out its public debt difficulties.

## National defaults likely

Full analysis of private and public debt levels reveals a major
chance of national and/or banking system default in Portugal,
Ireland and Greece, and a significant chance in Spain. For the
Euroland countries, the normal escape route of devaluation has
been cut off. But deflation without its normal accompaniment of
a cheaper currency thwarts the possibility of debt being mitigated
by economic growth – except for Ireland, which is competitive
now within the euro – and by inflation. Moreover, the natural
solution of quitting the euro has been made much harder by
most of the vulnerable countries accepting huge flows of cheap
funding from the ECB. To leave the euro would thus ensure
default anyhow, as the banking systems of the countries suffering
chiefly from excessive private-sector debt would find themselves
unable to fund their assets, forcing liquidation and massive losses
in a fire sale.

Leaving the euro would clearly be desirable in terms of ensuring some future growth, but these countries have made themselves so dependent on the stronger Euroland countries that
quitting EMU could only be done in the aftermath of default.

Even then it would be difficult to pull off unless the default, and write-down of obligations, had been on a sufficient scale to make future funding less than vital (as default plus euro exit would spell the end of financial market access for a while). It is unlikely that any of the countries involved have the intention of proceeding in such a fashion – they are all claiming to be committed to avoid default altogether – and neither do they have the guile to pull it off. The result is likely to be continued crisis. The best solution for Greece, for example, would be full default, exit from the euro and a support programme from the IMF alone. But the whole exercise would have to be negotiated with EMU as well, in order to permit orderly support for Euroland banks from its governments and the ECB, and orderly separation of euro from 'new drachma' assets and liabilities in Greece itself.

Just to outline such a programme indicates what a corner EMU has painted itself into. What has happened so far in the Euroland financial crisis looks more like the hors d'oeuvres than the main course – with probably more than one default, and nil to negative real economic growth in Club Med countries, though not Ireland, for a decade – especially if they do not make the break from EMU. The over-ambitious exercise in attempted continental unity could cause huge economic damage for a generation, with major risk of full-scale Depression.

# 6

# German confusion and fallacies

The problems of Ireland and Club Med arise not just from their own profligate behaviour and policies, but also from poor growth in Germany, despite its welcome two-year recovery 'bounce' since early 2009. This had brought real German GDP back to its pre-crisis peak by early 2011. Good German growth should persist until end-2011. It reflects excellent export growth, notably to China. The Chinese economy seems likely to slow significantly this year, and sharply next. But the US recovery has also been stronger than Germany's, and its probable acceleration under the impact of a cap-ex upsurge in late-2011 should specially favour Germany's capital goods-orientated industry. It should also sustain world trade growth, into which cost-competitive Germany sells well.

Before considering prospects, however, it is important to understand how Germany's weak growth in the cycle after the 2001 recession (ending with the crisis) contributed to the distortions that have culminated in the current disasters in Ireland and Club Med. As Figure 22 shows, the poor performance of German GDP (only 10% cumulative growth in nine years) looks rosy by comparison with the utterly dismal sluggishness of consumer spending. This particularly weak domestic demand has trebly undermined Euroland 'partners'.

Figure 22 **German real GDP and consumer spending**
*2001 Q4 = 100*

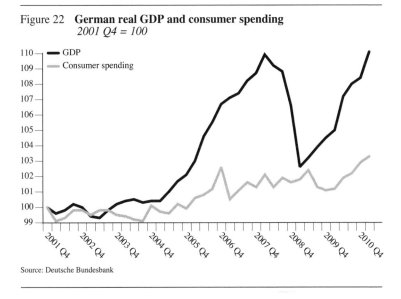

Source: Deutsche Bundesbank

Wages were aggressively repressed from 2002 onward, by severe fiscal tightening and heavy use of the threat of low-cost labour in central-eastern Europe, to restore 'competitiveness'. In reality, though labour cost measures showed German labour to be some 20% overpriced in the mid-1990s, much of that had disappeared by the euro's inception in 1999, as the trade-weighted DM had a 10% devaluation between 1995 and 1998. In the late 1990s and early in the last decade Germany did well in world trade share, despite the growing Chinese onslaught, so its export industries were clearly adjusted, in product quality, marketing, etc, to the initial EMU relative cost structure. It follows that the asserted need for cost cuts was not so much a national economic imperative (as it was presented) but simply a desirable improvement of the supply side that would raise productivity, income growth and hence general economic welfare. This, as we shall see, it did not do.

The effect of the 2002–05 deflation of the domestic German economy was to cut wages, and therefore consumer incomes. Combined with a higher savings rate – both for demographic reasons (p. 165–6 below) and because German consumers rightly thought the euro was and is a mechanism for Club Med to take the money out of their pockets – this led to negligible growth in real consumer spending. And wage repression meant German businesses became more *cost* competitive than their fellow EMU members (despite the slowing of productivity growth) gaining market share and sucking demand out of the rest of the world. So hammering wages both enabled German business to 'eat off the plates' of Euroland rivals and cut into what should have compensated for Germany's gains in market share: consumers spending the proceeds of their labours. These proceeds were instead funnelled into huge current account surpluses, invested abroad – and largely wasted (eg, in subprime US mortgage instruments and Greek government bonds). A third way in which German performance aggravated Euroland imbalances was that the slow growth in Europe's core kept euro interest rates low, boosting the debt-fuelled spree in the periphery, and contributing to the distortion in favour of real estate and construction.

Rosy commentary and forecasts for Germany generally ignore these damaging effects of its past policy and assume that the repression of wages and labour-market reforms will now ensure good growth. But the post-crisis recovery so far mostly reflects Germany's lack of inhibition by a debt hangover, as well as artificially competitive exports courtesy of EMU. Will it last in the face of the sharp slowdown likely in 2012, not only in China and the US, but also (importantly for still-European Germany) in

Club Med, Ireland and Britain, all of which are engaged in violent fiscal deflation?

Optimists on Germany claim that the slow growth of the last cycle (2001–09, measuring from one recession year to the next) saw a tremendous gain in the flexibility of the economy, arising from the fierce fiscal deflation of 2002–05 that crushed wages – with the help of threats to move jobs to countries such as Hungary – reinforced by the mid-decade Hartz labour-market reforms that increased flexibility in hiring and firing. But this faith in supply-side flexibility as a precursor of sustained growth, despite the threat of a global slowdown to demand growth in export-reliant Germany, ignores at least three other factors:

1. The chief beneficiary of the labour-market flexibility has been business profits, and, more generally, a shift away from labour income's share of GDP to profit income. It follows that demand will only emerge to ensure growth if either business cap-ex is boosted as a result of this greater profitability or (stimulated by low labour costs) employment continues to grow strongly.

2. The danger of persistent consumer spending weakness – a conspicuous feature of the 2001–09 cycle – arises not just because of labour income erosion in favour of profits. The household savings rate is high and has good reason at least to stay high, more likely to go higher, owing to demographic trends, widespread resentment of potential long-term German subsidies for Club Med and Ireland, and the rising German inflation that is inherent to its cost undervaluation and recent rapid, above-trend growth.

3. Depressingly, the supply-side 'reforms' have been accompanied by a major *slowing* of productivity growth, removing the whole basis of the argument that an improved supply side will enhance growth.

On a trend basis, Germany's 7½-year moving average growth rate
of output/worker-hour has fallen from 2–2¼% in the 1990s to ¾%
at the latest measure. More concretely, 2011 Q1 GDP was 0.1%
higher than the pre-crisis peak of 2008 Q1, yet employment was
1.6% higher. As well as the recovery being weaker than in debt-
burdened America, this means output per worker *fell* 1½% over the
three years in question – hardly the widely proclaimed economic
'miracle'.

Taking the last point first, Figure 23 shows that German productivity growth has lagged behind Britain's by nearly ½% a year
for nearly two decades (the past 11 years in Figure 23 plus the 7½
years covered by the moving average) and even further behind
America's over the past ten years. It is notable that its productivity
did better in the 1990s, the decade of adjustment to reunification,
than in the past ten years, the decade of euro-blight. Globally,
Germany is only cost-competitive because of its undervaluation
within the euro structure. The euro's exchange rate reflects only
partly German relative costs – it is biased down to compensate for
higher relative costs in Club Med and elsewhere. Poor productivity growth since Germany's early-2008 pre-crisis peak may be
partly caused by output shifting somewhat toward consumer and
other domestic-facing products, where Germany is less efficient.
Nonetheless, of the 1½% drop in output per employee over the
intervening three years, only ½% reflects shorter hours, the bulk
of the decline, 1%, being in output per hour worked, the fundamental measure of productivity.

In no way can the current recovery proceed like this without
raising inflationary pressures. Growth concentrated on higher
employment rather than productivity means unemployment is

Figure 23 **Output/worker-hour, whole economy**
*7½-year moving average, % pa*

Source: Deutsche Bundesbank, UK National Statistics and US Bureau of Labor Statistics
German and UK data are GDP/hour-worked. US is ⁴/₅ of the growth rate for non-farm business, given roughly
a 20% government employment ratio to the total.

already probably below its inflation-neutral rate – in fact it is the
lowest since reunification. Lombard Street Research computes
the 'output gap' for major economies, the difference between
actual output and its 'potential' or trend, and a positive output
gap indicates overheating in the economy, a negative gap slack.
Germany's output gap on this basis was a positive ½% in the last
quarter of 2010, and rose to 1¾–2% in 2011 Q1. At this level it
makes accelerating domestic inflation highly likely. The problem
partly results from the trend growth rate being around 1%: demand
can easily be excessive for such a slow-growth supply side. With
hourly productivity growth of ¾%, using the cyclically adjusted
7½-year average, falling average weekly hours, and employment
growth whose past trend has been about ¼%, this low trend is
no statistical surprise. But if the post-crisis result persists, with

hourly productivity actually down, or something in between, ie, very little growth, then the trend growth rate could even fall well short of 1%.

One aspect of these numbers is that Germany's undervalued real exchange rate and tendency over time to generate export demand will imply that non-inflationary growth is only possible with indefinite stagnation of consumer spending. But it may be that Germany's productivity outside of the exporters is even weaker than overall, so that it will be the gains in German consumer spending, needed to give much hope of any general European growth, that will ensure this feared result of even poorer productivity growth than in the past. Either way, the results from the German economy give no support to the view that some favourable structural reform has raised the likely growth in future from the poor performance of the past decade. On this analysis, the recovery to match the pre-crisis peak is just that. After continued good growth to end-2011, on the back of global strength, weak supply trends in the economy will be as strong a reason for weakness in 2012 and subsequent years as sluggish demand.

## Germany's inflation problem

It is inherent to the imbalances within EMU – now that they have led to crisis – that the undervalued portion of the bloc will tend to be inflated, and the overvalued portion deflated. Thus will tend to reverse the source of those imbalances: EMU's first ten years of higher inflation in Club Med. The logic is similar to that applied to the trans-Pacific dollar zone, Chimerica. Undervalued China was tending to inflation, and the overvalued US to deflation, until the Fed offset that with QE2 and loaded the entire imbalance onto Chinese inflation. Whereas in Chimerica, US control of the dollar taps means this duality is now biased toward Chinese inflation, in Europe the undervalued core, led by Germany, calls the shots. So the policies adopted are designed to rebalance the continent by deflation in the overvalued Club Med, with no inflation in Germany. But this intention looks as if it could be thwarted, at least until the Euroland economy falls back into recession, probably in 2012.

Two forces point toward inflationary dangers in Germany. Less important is the cost–push inflation arising for Germany, as with China, from the recent bout of US quantitative easing, 'QE2'. More important is that any sort of significant growth for the Euroland economy in aggregate, given Club Med domestic recession and limited locomotive power in France and Benelux, depends on Germany growing at 2% or more during 2011, ie, at ½% a quarter. In fact, of course, 2011 Q1 alone produced growth of 1½%, a 6% annual rate. Yet 2% annual growth rate in Germany, coming on top of the good recent recovery, which has put its GDP nearly 2% above trend, could quickly lead to overheating and domestically generated inflation.

German inflation would, of course, contribute both to rebalancing within the euro, and needed overall economic growth in Euroland. But that could come at the expense of further injury to the morale of the typical German consumer – whose reaction could then cut back the needed upswing of consumption. Already we have seen that the continuation of EMU with all its current members will probably, under *any* scenario, involve huge subsidies of Club Med countries, largely by Germany, for what is likely to be decades. If in addition Germans should have to bear inflation accelerating as the flip-side of deflation of Club Med demand, the divisions within Europe could shift even more violently than is already threatened from economic to political.

Already, the cost–push element has affected German inflation, and even the demand–pull element is beginning to show. On the cost–push side, the upswing of food and energy prices induced by QE2 – which has lowered real incomes in the US, and done so strongly in China – has affected Germany (as well as the rest of Europe). But some of the sting has been taken out of this effect by the rise of the euro, which corresponds to the inflation-driven rise in the real exchange rate of the Chinese yuan, and is an essential part of the global adjustment needed to achieve rebalancing.

It is at the level of domestic costs and prices that, by sacrificing its currency and monetary-policy autonomy, Germany has lost its ability to pursue one of its citizens' primary goals: stable prices. So far this has mostly shown in the area leading Germany's brisk recovery: manufacturing. The PPI ex-energy had a 4% 12-month increase in spring 2011 – a major 7½ percent-point swing from its end-recession decline nearly two years earlier. This 4% non-energy goods price inflation is 1% clear of its highest inflation rate since the pre-reunification 1980s. At the consumer level, ex-energy inflation has so far only accelerated from ¾% in late-summer 2010 to 1½% in spring, 2011, but that acceleration occurred despite the economy only becoming overheated, in the sense of output being above its trend, in late-2010. With the overheating getting substantially greater in early 2011, both manufactured goods prices and ex-energy consumer price inflation could go higher.

## Poor 2012 German growth outlook

Sadly, enduring German inflation problems arising from strong consumer spending growth is not the most likely scenario. Coming on top of general weakness in Europe, extreme in Club Med, poor US growth prospects in 2012 and a sharp Chinese slowdown augur badly for German exporters, for whom the Chinese market is the 'great white hope'. Meanwhile, the government intends to tighten the budget balance by about ½% of GDP of policy measures. In a US or British context this might not sound like much (let alone by comparison with current savage Club Med and Irish deflation) but for Germany, with a trend growth rate probably below 1%, it is substantial. While domestic capital goods orders are buoyant, indicating that this year's export surge will lead to some knock-on effect in capital spending, any longevity for the recent recovery must depend on that deeply unreliable agent, the German consumer.

Optimists may boost the prospects for German consumption, but have little grounds for their belief. It is true that the decade-long increase of the saving rate, from close to 10% in 1999 to close to 12% at times in 2008–09, seems to have stopped. (Figure 24). But it would be rash to suggest any major decline is imminent. The German baby boom did not get going until the 1950s, and the early-60s age-group shortly due to reach 'retirement age' is by a long way the smallest of the last century, given millions of people killed at the end of the Second World War and intense hardship in its immediate aftermath that cut into births. So no surge of people shifting to low savings rates after retirement is even on the cards for some five to seven years. On the contrary, the peak German age group is in its mid-to-late 40s – the baby

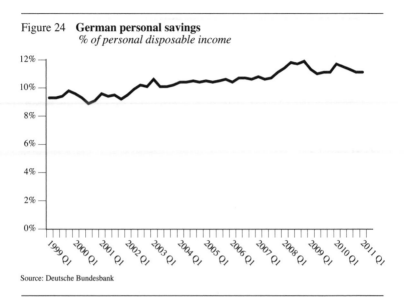

Figure 24 **German personal savings**
*% of personal disposable income*

Source: Deutsche Bundesbank

boom continued until the early 1970s – and is likely to be increasing its savings rate in life-cycle terms over the next few years – all the more so if they are anxious about relying on state pensions.

When it comes to the upward pressure on savings from the prospect of decades of subsidy to Club Med and Ireland, Chancellor Merkel provides the best measure. As the Greek crisis forced the initial subsidy plan in May, 2010, she unilaterally cancelled in public the intended tax cuts that were part of the coalition agreement with her Free Democrat partners, and had been a cardinal part of their political and economic programme. The reason given was that the need to subsidise Greece meant that Germany could no longer afford tax cuts. Needless to state, exactly the opposite is the truth: because of the dire deflation being imposed on Club Med and Ireland, both Europe in general and Germany in particular needed greater demand stimulation in financially unconstrained Germany. But Mrs Merkel's reaction gives a clear indication that the continuing subsidies needed for Southern Europe will also contribute to weak consumer demand in Germany, as anxious housewives close their purses.

The last, though probably ephemeral, inhibition on German consumers could be inflation. This is a natural result of an under-valued currency in a world of reasonable growth overall – ie, the world of 2010 and 2011. German people hate inflation for sound historic reasons, though the conditions of 1923–24 that produced hyperinflation were special and highly unlikely to be reproduced. It has to be likely, however, that accelerating inflation in 2011 will slow German consumer spending (ie, raise savings) at a key moment – the transition from strong world trade to severe weakness in 2012. In the probable Euroland recession of 2012 German inflation should wane. Sadly, by then an inflation-induced rise in savings could be overtaken by weakness of consumer incomes. The result will remain the same: little German real consumer spending growth in future, just like the past.

## The fallacy of long-term German policy

Aside from a pathological obsession with government deficits, Germany policy is based on a view of the country's future, and how to deal with it, that seems profoundly flawed. The basic argument is that the decline in the number of Germans of working age and the large generation due to have retired by, say, 20 years from now, requires the country to postpone consumption to generate and save up huge balance of payments surpluses to provide future income when the output of that reduced labour force is overburdened by the spending needs of the retired people. It sounds like common sense, but the assumptions are weak or plain wrong at a number of points:

1. Working age is not stable. People are healthier and longer-lived all the time. They do not like the sharp drop in income and activity that comes with retirement. In all advanced economies the ratio of workers in the over-65s is soaring. Labour force participation in Germany has been rising in the under-65 age group too.
2. This factor both severely qualifies the potential drop in the labour force *and* cuts the potential growth of dependent old people.
3. When Central and Eastern European (CEE) countries entered the EU in May 2004, there was a seven-year block on their citizens working in the 'old' EU. This was waived by Britain, Ireland and Sweden. This moratorium ran out in May 2011. Poland, the largest CEE country, is 60 miles from Berlin. Migration could be vigorous in the next few years.
4. Basing the future on earning trade surpluses has, associated with biasing the real exchange rate downwards, meant a steady worsening of the German terms of trade, ie, the buying power of German product, so that its full value is not reflected in either the current or future potential income of German citizens.
5. Such surpluses earned by excessive German saving after allowance for point 4 above are badly invested – with major losses in US subprime mortgages, Greek government bonds, etc. This will continue as the surpluses depend on continuation of German undervaluation in EMU that in turn depends on Club-Med overvaluation and their resulting dependence on German subsidies (or 'investments').
6. Aside from obvious wastage as per point 5, Germany has had a similar steady erosion of the labour share of GDP to Japan, with

similar implications of excessive corporate income that is then disbursed without sufficient discipline.

7. Together with the most efficient sector of the economy, exports, being cosseted by low costs within EMU, this too-easy accession of profit income has led to loss of discipline and contributed to the fall in productivity growth.

8. The loss of growth from German self-restraint has spilled over to poor supply-side performance for a variety of reasons, depressing the income level from which both current and future consumption has to be financed. A more uninhibited approach to spending and growth could raise the level of income from which some future, demographically driven phase of slower growth might start, thereby improving prospects for Germans, both current and future. Put another way, current versus future spending is probably a positive-sum, not a zero-sum, game.

In the ten years from 1998 to 2008, the labour force grew 3% while the population aged 19–64 fell 3%, a combined divergence of 6%, 0.6% a year. Reinforcing this is the point on p. 165 above that the 60–65 year-old age-group, born in 1945–50, is extremely small in Germany, owing to the desperate post-Second World War conditions. This means those who would normally be expecting to retire in the next five years are fewer than the age-group coming into the labour force for the first time for a decade or so (a situation that will not persist much beyond 2015). So for the medium term the working-age population measured 'old-style', ie, 16–64s or 20–64s, will be tending to increase, leaving aside extra boosts to the labour force from rising participation and over-65s continuing to hang onto their jobs – or at least continuing to work, if elsewhere at lesser pressure and/or income.

The much feared decline of the labour force could be at least a decade off, if not more, just at the indigenous level, leaving aside migration. Onto this by no means declining demographic trend must be grafted what may be a substantial likely inflow of people from CEE countries, both those there now and some of those who have already migrated to Britain, Ireland and Sweden simply because they have been the countries open to CEE people. Ireland in particular is a likely source, given the savage deflation now being vented on it. As the net migration from this source to Britain has formed the bulk of the net immigration of 200,000 for-eigners a year, the potential impact of this factor on the German labour force, currently of the order of 40 million, is large.

Aside from the folly of assuming as certain such a specula-tive factor as a declining labour force, the policy of undervaluing the currency to secure export-led growth shows naturally dimin-ishing returns. German export prices have been falling short of import prices by an average ½% a year for the past 20 years. The cumulative shortfall is 10%, in contrast to stable terms of trade in the US (despite greater dependence on oil prices, which have been rising) and rising terms of trade in Britain (which is oil-neutral owing to the North Sea). This erosion of the relative value of exports translates directly into reduced buying power for the surpluses being built up supposedly to finance the incomes of future dependent, aged Germans.

When it comes to investment of the surpluses built up at such cost, the German record is not consistent with the strategy of providing future income for a large, dependent age-group. The current account moved into surplus again from its post-reunifica-tion deficits in 2001, and the cumulative total of current surpluses over the ten years to 2010 was €1.050 billion. But the change in the net overseas investment position of Germany between the end of 2000 and 2010 was only €982 billion. The return on capital was negative, by 7% in total on an average outstanding period of four years or so (most of the surpluses being earned in the latter half of the decade). Obviously, US mortgages and Greek government bonds played a part in this. In real buying power, the fall in value of the net external assets was obviously greater, given inflation.

A contributory factor to both the worsening terms of trade and poor overseas returns could be the feather-bedding of industry by undervaluation, courtesy of the euro. One result is that the labour income share of GDP has been falling for 20 years. In the old days before the euro, this redistribution would have been offset by a rising exchange rate leading to downward pressure on profits, and upward valuation of real wages and salaries, as wage repression improved cost competitiveness. It might be argued that the wage share was too high in the early 1990s after German reunification. But the German ratio is well below that of the US and Japan, and the downward trend has re-asserted itself after the backing up of this ratio in the recession. (Recessions always hit profits harder than wages in the short run.)

Within the euro, the steady gains in unit labour costs in the other EMU countries has ensured that German labour does not get its just reward for restraint of wages, but that the spending power is siphoned off into business – which does not need it, of course, as the stagnation of overall population and upward shift of capital productivity in the 2002–05 period resulted in a downward trend in the investment share of GDP. The danger of such easy times for business cash flow is weaker discipline in the use of cash, much of which necessarily flowed abroad, and this may well have been one cause of the downward trend in productivity growth.

## Will Germany be harmed if EMU breaks up?

Germany is as likely to see faster growth as slower in anything but the very short term, if it quits EMU. The cumulative distortions of 12 years of EMU are not confined to Club Med. EMU's sacrifice of German consumers in favour of its exporters and business cash balances has had the severe effects already itemised above. But leaving the euro would lead to a large, rapid gain in real consumer incomes as the new German currency would appreciate. In addition, the fear of inflation would be sharply reduced, and the burden of supporting countries that obviously need devaluation likewise (not least because they would effectively get devaluation through the upward German float). A longer-term supply-side point is that German industry would get some badly needed cost discipline to enforce productivity gains, in contrast to the feather-bedding they have received within EMU from suppression of wages – ie, ordinary Germans' incomes.

The experience of Germany in the 1970s, when it outperformed most other industrial economies despite a rapidly rising real exchange rate, suggests that the short-term competitiveness effects of a rising real exchange rate can soon be offset. And a higher exchange rate would probably cause a healthy redistribution of income from business to labour, ie, consumers – the lack of which is closely connected to undervaluation and excess savings and net export surpluses in Japan and China, as well as Germany. Since Germany is unlikely to follow China's route of real exchange rate appreciation by means of wage inflation, giving some possibility of a shift to consumption from exports, a break-up of EMU may actually be the only hope for achieving an increase of welfare for ordinary Germans. What seems clear is that if EMU survives with all its present countries, those ordinary Germans will have to pay much larger subventions for the sake of European unity over the next 20 years than those paid to East Germany for German reunification over the past 20.

# 7

# Islands apart – Japan and Britain

Table 2 (p. 144 above) shows that the global leaders in excess debt amongst G-7 economies (ie, away from Club Med and Ireland but amongst major advanced economies) are Japan and Britain. Japan is more immediately exposed owing to its debt being concentrated in the public sector – and liable to cause more trouble even than the high, 110% of GDP, ratio might suggest, as gross government debt is 200% of GDP. Both economies have the advantage of genuinely floating exchange rates, which take a substantial portion of the strain of adjustment to changing global conditions. But both have major drawbacks aside from their excessive debt levels: over-reliance on exports in Japan's case (a chronic deficiency of domestic demand vis-à-vis potential supply), and proximity to hobbled Euroland in Britain's.

## Japan's deepest problem: maldistribution of income

Japan's crucial weakness is the maldistribution of income – not between rich and poor, but between businesses and households. Personal disposable income in the US is 15 percentage points of gross domestic product higher than in Japan. Yet the two countries have about the same size public sectors, so that is not the source of the difference, as it is between the US and Western Europe. Business depreciation is 21% of Japanese GDP, versus 12% in the US. Essentially, Japanese business hogs a grotesquely large flow of tax-free depreciation – owing to decades of wasteful overinvestment and poor income growth – which it refuses to distribute. The dividend yield only uses up one third of the significant earnings that remain after the artificially large deduction for depreciation.

Japan's personal savings rate is roughly comparable with the US, but the low share of personal income in gross domestic income (= GDP in principle) means consumption is structurally too low. Wasteful business investment, large structural government deficits and persistent over-reliance on exports offset inadequate consumer spending, perpetuating the depreciation problem, the deficiency of domestic demand vis-à-vis potential output, and hence, via the resulting deflation combined with government deficits, indefinitely rising government debt. Contributing to low consumption in the resulting deflationary economy is the low rate of interest that ensures Japanese households, with a massive 1½ times GDP in bank deposits (2½ times disposable income), receive no interest income.

In these circumstances, Japan has a flat to declining nominal GDP, comprising rather under 1% trend growth and rather more than 1% deflation. (Current GDP levels were first achieved, grown through and therefore last seen, in 1991.) As the business sector's structural surplus has to be offset at least partially by government deficits – the other outlet, overseas surplus, being limited – it follows that the debt load mounts without apparent limit. At end-2010, government net debt was 110% of GDP, with its gross debt of 200% offset by considerable assets, not least 20% of GDP in foreign exchange reserves. While Japanese household debt is modest, its NFC debt is non-trivial at 2½ times EBITDA (the best comparator for Japan) and its overall non-financial debt ratio to GDP is level with Spain and the UK, and well above the US. The prospect is that government debt steadily grows until a crisis emerges, owing to some (inevitably unforeseeable) contingency.

It is a tragic irony that the March 2011 disasters – earthquake, tsunami and nuclear near melt-down – could change this self-obstructing stasis in perversely useful ways. It is unlikely that output will be severely hit or disrupted for long, either in Japan itself, or further afield. Industrial production in the four prefectures close to Sendai and Fukushima was 7½% of Japan's total, and they are distinguished by small and medium-sized enterprises (SMEs) rather than major firms in what is a relatively rural region. Capacity utilisation in Japan just before the earthquake was 7½% below its normal level. As the four prefectures are far from fully closed down, after a short period of adjustment in March and the second quarter, output has recovered. The effects of the disasters are boosting demand in the latter part of this year, as reconstruction gets under way, as well as clearly having cut into productive capacities a little, with GDP if anything higher than it would have been without the disasters.

Importantly, the yen is weakened. Households are likely to become nervous about investments in Japan, especially real estate. Business too will wish to have adequate overseas facilities to ensure continuity of output in the event of further disasters. Meanwhile, the Bank of Japan has quite reasonably provided liquidity, lowering short-term interest rates – low though they already were. This can only favour money-market outflows. A weakening of the yen should add to demand and raise the possibility of inflation.

The effects of the disasters, therefore, involve a clear and desirable tightening of the domestic Japanese demand/supply balance, plus some improvement of export demand. It is possible this could lead to a virtuous circle, driven by stronger demand. One fear is that because much of the reconstruction spending is government funded, it will add to an already excessive government deficit. This illustrates the point that it could well be the onset of recovery that provokes the almost inevitable sell-off in Japanese government bonds (JGBs). If deflation were to give way to stable prices, there would be little justification for the current JGB yields of 1¼% for ten-year paper.

The upside of a JGB sell-off and the end of deflation could be positive interest rates, so that those huge household bank deposits would yield improved personal income and probably consumption. The downside risk, of course, is that losses on JGBs might inhibit GDP through a negative wealth effect, and the government, fearing an upsurge in its financing costs, could cut back its deficit – probably prematurely, on past form – hammering domestic demand yet again. It is impossible to forecast convincingly when the JGB crisis will hit – and how – but only a sharp shift in corporate behaviour toward distribution of earnings as dividends can prevent it happening some time, perhaps quite soon. Only if companies slash their financial surplus can the government tighten its fiscal stance without the economy relapsing and provoking a new round of government deficits.

## Britain: household debt excess and supply-side adjustment

Britain's medium-term growth is bound to be inhibited by a number of factors (not listed in order of importance here):

1. Demand side:
   a. strong retrenchment of the government deficit;
   b. the need for household debt ratios to be cut;
   c. feeble to non-existent growth in continental Europe.
2. Supply side:
   a. smaller financial services sector in the medium term;
   b. shift to newly profitable sectors via devaluation inhibited by their past shrinkage;
   c. weakening of London real estate by Pacific-region/oil-producer wealth losses.

The demand-side points above interact with one another, with monetary policy as the crucial agency of this interaction – hence the vital solvent of a floating exchange-rate that permits an independent monetary policy, meaning national solvency is not an issue, and not likely to be. Taking (a) and (b) first, the analysis of debt ratios in the Appendix strongly suggests that the British household debt ratio, above 160% of gross disposable income, though less absurdly high than Ireland, needs to come down. Yet what makes it tolerable at the moment is the Bank of England (BoE) setting the banks' base rate at ½%, effectively nil. With floating-rate household mortgages (the bulk of the debt) only costing 3½% as a result, households are able to sustain their debt service. Both the relatively high inflation rate, mostly reflecting past devaluation since 2007, and the need for further real exchange rate reductions to ensure supply-side shifts and growth led by net exports (as in the US case), suggest interest rates will be higher over time. This implies that households will have their disposable income significantly cut by higher mortgage interest rates, offsetting the demand benefit from devaluation.

The argument against this is that fiscal retrenchment is so strong that even in a context of devaluation and continued above-target inflation the BoE will keep rates low, postponing (at least to some degree) household debt reduction. And the scale of devaluation and continued inflationary pressure may be raised by the feeble growth prospects in continental Europe, which comprises about half Britain's export market. Exports are themselves 30% of GDP, ie, some 22–23% of total demand (= GDP + imports). As British inflation reflects devaluation, ie, higher import prices, it also potentially reduces real household incomes, further inhibiting demand. So the medium term contains these three self-reinforcing waves of demand restraint – sharply tighter government budgets, eventual household debt reduction through a higher savings rate, and curbs on household real incomes by import-price-led inflation and possibly higher interest rates if recovery is at all satisfactory.

On the plus side for demand, supply-side adjustment arising from past and likely future cuts in the real exchange rate should take the form not just of improved net exports, but also higher business investment. So far, the devaluation of sterling has not led to the expected major downward shift of the terms of trade, export prices vis-à-vis import prices. While the higher import prices have worsened real household incomes, the business sector has mostly taken the benefit in the form of higher profit margins, rather than cutting prices to make UK exports more cost-competitive. This has shown itself in strong profits, a major increase in the cash flow surplus over capital spending and inventory costs, and a rapid cut in business debt ratios.

The long-term shrinkage of British manufacturing means much of it is in specialised fields with high import content. Devaluation naturally tends to show in profit margins rather than lesser prices, which are set globally by international competitors. But the strong profits and cash flow are likely to mean significant strengthening of investment to take advantage of the good return on capital. By this route the economy should, from a supply-side perspective, achieve a rebalancing that compensates over time for the loss of income from financial services, and business services generally. Nor is the latter likely to be as drastic as recent data might suggest. While medium-term weakness of banking value-added is as likely in Britain as in the US (see p. 44 above), the wholesale financial services that the City of London specialises in have seen their downswing exaggerated by their inherent cyclicality – in a global down-cycle that has, of course, been the worst since the Second World War. In a less drastically repressed (though hardly buoyant) medium-term global environment, British business services, with the labour-cost advantage of devaluation, should be able to recapture much of the lost ground.

One major 'shoe yet to drop', however, is the danger that the cash flow to London as the destination of choice for the world's funk money is likely to diminish. This is not chiefly a function of changes in taxation, though these may have some impact on location choices for firms and rich individuals. The chief point is that most of the money comes from East and South-East Asia, including China, and the Middle East, notably oil exporters, together with Russia, also oil-dependent. And the forecast here is that all these groups will be very substantially less well off in future than in the recent and current booms in emerging Asian economies and energy and other commodity prices. Once the top end of the London real estate and service industries feels a significantly slower flow of 'offshore' income, the effects will reverberate down the chain, partly in the volume of activity, but mostly in the prices that can be charged.

The overall picture for Britain is one of very moderate growth in the medium term. With a cyclically adjusted growth trend of 1% in hourly productivity, the growth of employment would normally be contributing some ¾%, with some loss of weekly hours over time, for a GDP trend of some 1½%. But a more realistic forecast for the 3–5 year medium term could be 1%. Compared to the US, Britain has a larger household debt problem, with less deleverage so far, a larger financial sector to shrink, and an uncomfortable dependence on hobbled Euroland. And any growth could be 'feel-bad' growth, owing to worse terms of trade. The fall in oil prices to be expected will not help the British terms of trade, owing to small net oil imports. Further devaluation is likely to erode the terms of trade. A weakening of London real estate in response to global wealth losses could knock on to another substantial downswing in house prices generally, increasing the pressure on households from excessive debts. Britain's prospects are less bleak than on the continent, but much worse than over the 15 years to 2007.

# 8

# Is there *any* hope?

This is a gloomy book, highlighting plenty of dangers. The basic story is that people and governments only change their ways when previous habits cause them pain – severe enough pain to overcome the perceived risks of change. This book continues a series in which the excess savings habit is fingered as the primary economic cause of the imbalances and the 2007–09 crisis. It argues that this habit has not been abandoned – or even acknowledged as damaging to a large extent – by its perpetrators, most conspicuously Germany and China. It is only through their pain that a remedy for the world's ills will emerge. That is human nature. So this is a gloomy book. The thick layers of German self-righteousness and economic ignorance, and Chinese bluff and denial, will not be torn away easily. China and Europe seems set for a very rough decade.

Let us consider what is concluded here in relation to what we assert are the mainstream views of various countries' and other prospects:

1. Moderately better than consensus: US (whose growth could be on-trend though not booming, but has a major downswing to go through next year).

2. About the same as consensus: Japan, Britain (both with moderately unfavourable prospects) and emerging markets that are not unduly commodity-dependent and can generate growth by means of domestic demand.

3. Moderately worse than consensus: India (so far unmentioned) because of its self-generated inflation problem, and Ireland and Club Med (as most commentators are only part of the way to understanding how bleak their prospects are).

4. Much worse than consensus: China (whose growth is likely to halve over the next decade, with strong political danger attached), Germany (whose growth after 2011 could return to negligible) and 'hard' commodity prices and the countries that depend on exporting them.

To finish off on the gloom, it is worth pointing out that the major stress forecast here for the US economy over the next year, and the world economy for the next five, is likely to involve largely unpredictable, but almost certainly negative, economic and political risks. At the political level the most obvious danger, given the essentially deflationary nature of the prospects, is a return to that bane of the 1930s – narrow nationalism. It is hard to see the prospects for Club Med not leading to some form of political break-down in one of the four countries involved. It is possible that Germany could swing into a much more nationalistic political frame, throwing out much of the 'baby' of European integration and the single market with the 'bathwater' of euro-folly. Germans are, after all, about to be asked to subsidise Club Med for 20 years at a cost greater than that of subsidising East Germany for the past 20. And at least East Germany was incorporated into a formal political union with West Germany before that started, in contrast with the ill thought-out shambles that is the so-called 'Economic and Monetary Union'. It would be hard not to sympathise with Germans who finally kicked over the traces.

Perhaps even more seriously, but also more speculatively, there are many commentators who believe that the kind of stresses that China could come under will have highly unstable political consequences – though the true internal politics of that country are too obscure for anything more than speculation. And the US itself, despite its better medium-term prospects, is quite capable of responding to the grim forecast we are making for 2012 (if it turns out that way) with some form of spectacular national tantrum. In which case ... Watch out, rest of world! Nor does the likelihood of much lower oil prices over the medium term stack up well against the instability suddenly emerging from the 'Arab Spring'. Existing oil-exporter regimes will be weakened, and the risks of political upset much enhanced – with no guarantees yet in place that the evident desire for democracy on the 'Arab street' will make democracy happen. A reversion to repression, like Europe after 1848, is quite possible, but any scenario has multiple possibilities for conflict.

To answer the question 'Is there any hope?' some positive points can be made. If the US gets through 2012 without too much upheaval, its brighter medium-term prospects will restore it to primacy in world affairs, and people will find that much more comfortable than the two-superpower alternative that appeared to be emerging. And US stocks and other risk assets could do well. If the Arab Spring does lead to the development of one or more genuine democracies, that statement of preference by Arabs may put paid to the idea that the world is inevitably drifting politically to some Chinese version of the 'Asian way'. And India, now embroiled in major inflation arising from years of thoroughly irresponsible fiscal policies, nonetheless has the scope over the medium term to continue growing at a 7–8% trend rate, and thus playing catch-up with China – in the process showing a major Asian version of a successful democracy. Meanwhile, other emerging economies without undue dependence on commodities may find themselves able to achieve sustained catch-up growth, helped by lower energy and metal prices. This group includes most of Latin America, notably Brazil and Mexico, and major countries such as Turkey and Indonesia. And then there are always the surprises – some of which are inevitably favourable ones.

But the basic message of this book is that the world as a whole has not faced up to the true nature of the crisis, which therefore has to repeat itself. This is not good news. What is good news is that America, the foundation stone of the world economy, should be the Phoenix that rises from the ashes of the forecast 2012 economic slump.

## Manifesto

It is a frequent comment on our work and conclusions that we should provide a set of recommendations to enable the world to avoid the gloomy future we are forecasting. Of course, the chief reason for the gloom of these forecasts is that the measures needed to avert the forecast trouble are in conflict with the attitudes and behaviour of the various different countries, these being the fundamental source of the problems. Put simplistically, for the trouble we expect to be avoided, China needs to stop being China, Germany Germany, Japan Japan, America America – and so forth. And they need to have stopped being themselves two to three years ago – now is not soon enough. The bust forecast for next year already looks set in concrete.

There is a deeper point concerning the need to change the attitudes and behaviour of the various nations. Nations do not change their more damaging ways in response to cool, external reasoning. They only change when their errors cause enough pain to overcome those entrenched attitudes and habits. In this sense, our gloom about the immediate future is an optimistic stance: if the pain is near at hand, the possibility of remedy is relatively immediate. Equally, slumps and other malign developments generally lead to policy blunders. And the politics of the hard times we are forecasting could bring about political changes that are worse than mere depression – as happened in the 1930s.

But in the interests of illustrating the changes and policies that might help mitigate the poor medium-term future forecast here, this book will end with a non-exhaustive list of changes that are needed under various headings. In the case of the US and Germany, the constitutional amendments suggested here illustrate how little chance there is of these recommendations being accepted.

## Excess saving

- China and Germany need to acknowledge that excess saving was the fundamental economic cause of the 2007–09 crisis, and that it continues to bedevil any chance of full global recovery.
- They further need to acknowledge that 2011's return to 2007's excessive world gross savings rate means that policies to cut government deficits, unaccompanied by deliberate reduction of excess saving in their economies, raises the likelihood of a global deficiency of

demand, given the degree of waste already evident in current rates of fixed investment.

- Based on these two points, they need to declare raising their consumption rates to be the primary goal of demand-management policy, and to submit every other policy to the test of whether it supports or frustrates this goal.
- All nations collectively need to acknowledge that shifting government deficits down to rates that stabilise debt ratios to income may have to proceed more gradually than is currently hoped and intended, owing to the probability of stubbornly high private sector surpluses for the medium term.

## *Full return to floating exchange rates*

- China needs to abandon all attempts to control its exchange rate, and set an objective of no change in its foreign exchange reserves.
- Euroland needs to shed Club Med and become a coherent bloc comprising Germany, Benelux, France and Austria (that could be joined by Denmark and/or Sweden once its current deeply suboptimal membership is rationalised).

## *Chinese policies*

- China should dismantle all controls on international capital movements.
- It should shift its monetary policy basis from the current administered control of lending by the government to market-based banking and rationing of credit by price, ie, free interest rates according to the credit quality of the borrower.
- It needs to accept market-driven closure of businesses that will find their economics worsened by increases in both the exchange rate and the interest rates.

- It needs to establish full freehold for farmers in their land, rather than the current state ownership with leases to farmers.
- It needs to permit free transfer of residence by its citizens between rural and urban areas, and around the country in general.
- It needs to implement more effective social security, covering pension, health and unemployment, for all sections of the population.

## US policies

- The US needs to shift the emphasis in upcoming public spending cuts away from 'muscle', ie, infrastructure, education and assistance to ensure development of the potential of children of poor families.
- Probably, such a shift will mean tackling entitlement programmes, such as Social Security and Medicare – most obviously by gradually increasing the age at which entitlement kicks in.
- It clearly needs higher energy taxes to reinforce lesser energy dependence in the economy, and a probable improvement of its terms of trade.
- The US should change its constitution to permit corporate lobbying to be regulated.

## Japanese policies

- Japan needs most of all to tackle corporate waste, and adopt policies to make companies disgorge profits to shareholders.

## Euroland policies

- Greece needs to default, quit the euro and call in the IMF for a proper, IMF-led deficit-reduction programme, rather than the current scheme where the IMF plays second-fiddle to politically motivated Euroland politicians.
- Portugal will probably need to follow Greece.

- Ireland will probably also need a debt write-down, but could survive within the euro in cost-competitive terms, but should probably leave, partly to have its own interest rates, rather than those suited to core Euroland, partly to reflect its three-way economic links to Euroland, the UK and the US.
- Spain, with 21% unemployment, 40% amongst youth, should quit the euro to avoid a decade of stagnation, as it grapples with excessive company debt, and to ensure its labour costs are highly competitive, making employment of Spanish labour attractive.
- Spain should dismantle job protection laws and index-linking of wages.
- A coherent Euroland based on Germany, France, Benelux and Austria will need a proto-Finance Ministry to give political heft to EMU financial policies that is currently being assumed arbitrarily by the ECB.

## German policies

- Economically, the interests of German citizens would be best served by quitting the euro, accepting a rising real exchange rate, and with it pressure on German business to cut costs and raise productivity, ensuring rising real incomes and spending for German consumers.
- Quitting the euro would satisfy one of the chief goals of the German public, eliminating inflation, and would reduce the need for future subsidy of Club Med after the scarring experience of 20 years' subventions to the former East Germany.
- Germany should accept that as long as its private sector is aiming for financial surplus anywhere near the current 8% of GDP, the public budget must remain in structural deficit, in the process repealing the recent constitutional amendment prohibiting such deficits.

# Appendix

## How much debt is sustainable?

D ebt arouses moral feelings, involving shame and guilt, as well as economic issues. Partly as a result, discussion of debt is often confused. But confusion also arises because the economics of debt is complex, with different implications for one type of debtor from another, whether the difference be in legal status (eg, household, private limited company, government), level of income, or purpose for which the borrowing is undertaken (eg, infrastructure, business equipment, housing, personal consumption, fiscal stimulus). This appendix will attempt to set up reasonable measures to judge affordability or sustainability of debt according to the borrower's status, taking account (where due) of the purpose of the borrowing, and different national habits and attitudes to debt. This analysis is the essential underpinning of the conclusions in earlier chapters of this book about which countries have a significant debt problem, and in what form.

The countries covered include the world's major developed economies that are widely said to have debt excesses, the US, Japan, the UK, Italy and Spain, and their data is compared to relatively well-placed Germany. Similar analytical criteria are applied to Greece, Ireland and Portugal (the other EMU 'problem children' along with Italy and Spain). China may well prove vulnerable to debt problems in future, also Australia, given its huge personal sector debt and persistent (and therefore evidently sustainable) current account deficits. But they, and the old bad-debtors of Latin America, will not be covered here. Fast growth increases debt capacity and, in China's case, the overall debt in the country (including private and public sectors) is in any case quite low. Australia, despite a strong growth trend by advanced country standards, does indeed have potential problems, but they spring in the first instance from the likely bear market in commodity prices over the next few years. While that may reveal serious household debt problems in particular, those will be secondary to this initial, primary problem.

## What is (are) the limit(s) of debt?

The desirable limit of debt in principle is the maximum amount that can be comfortably financed by the future flow of the debtor's income. This means the sustainable debt level is different for households from businesses. A household borrower should have the means to repay the debt over time – the alternative (in the case of a mortgage) of selling the house represents (at best) personal failure. Business debt up to a certain level can reasonably be expected to be 'rolled over', provided it is well covered by assets and/or the interest by cash flow. Government debt has a call on the entire flow of national income, via taxation.

The overall level of private-plus-public debt in a nation is also relevant, as an excess of debt in the private sector can quite quickly be transferred to the public sector, either directly – or indirectly as a result of fiscal and monetary policy, as has been evident over the past 2–3 years. So all debt can ultimately end up as a public responsibility – in which case, its overall level is a policy concern at all times. Warnings on this were aggressive from 2004 by Lombard Street Research as well as by many others, and the authorities' neglect in the face of such warnings was a major contributor to the 2007–09 crisis.

Household debt in principle has to be financed from labour income, though it is conventional to relate it to total disposable income of households. But households with significant capital (outside of the mortgaged house itself) and investment income tend to have no great burden of debt, though in some booms excessively leveraged positions in stock markets and other risky assets make an appearance. Most household debt takes the form of home mortgages, with consumer debt also significant. The relevant question is the affordability of total debt service, including repayment of principal, which is normally done over the bulk of a working lifetime in the case of mortgages, or a much shorter period for consumer debt – 2–3 years for hire-purchase (US: 'instalment') debt, less, one hopes, for credit card debt.

What about household assets – are they not relevant? Those with mortgages tend to have the bulk of their non-housing assets locked up in pension arrangements. So the value of the house is the chief relevant issue. And housing values did indeed mightily spur the take-up of mortgages until 2007. But in the US, the boom caused rising nominal interest rates after 2004, with falling house affordability, so that house prices peaked in spring 2006 and then turned down. When the subprime crisis hit in late 2007, the fall in house prices became a rout. At the exact moment when the value in houses was needed it ceased to be there! Why did prices fall? Because they were too high in relation to income.

This reinforces the point that it is from future income that house-hold debt must be serviced, not assets. Britain might appear to contradict this – its house prices fell in the crisis, but revived after early-2009. But that was chiefly because the predominance of floating-rate mortgages meant that interest rates slashed close to zero sharply cut debt service relative to income. Once again, it was the affordability of debt service from income that turned out to be the crucial issue.

Fixing the 'right ratio' of household debt to disposable income is subject to variations in national behaviour traits, which can themselves vary over time. Thus, for example, US household debt has proven to be excessive at a lower ratio to income than British and Australian. For the most part, this is not the result of higher interest rates – rather the contrary (nominal interest rates being the primary affordability criterion, not real rates). In addition, interest on US mortgage borrowing is usually tax deductible, unlike most other countries, making the amount payable out of disposable income significantly less. Their lower apparent sustainable debt ratio may partly be the result of Americans being habituated to spending a higher proportion of their after-tax incomes on goods and services, leaving less available for debt service.

Certainly, the predominance of fixed-rate mortgages in the US makes households more vulnerable in a recession, as mon-etary policy offers much less relief. But it was mortgage defaults that caused recession, rather than the other way round. A more unequal after-tax income distribution in the US, combined with greater job insecurity, also puts greater pressure on lower-income households, where debt service is most likely to cause financial problems. Lastly, US mortgages are generally secured on the property only, whereas elsewhere the lender generally also has an unsecured charge on the borrower that cannot be evaded by simply dumping the house back on the lender in lieu of loan repayment. US lenders are therefore in jeopardy at lower levels of household financial stress. As to change over time, the debt capacity of US households may have been seriously exceeded by the excesses of 2003–07, but it has been increasing over time as mortgage products improve and the end of the high inflation of the 1970s and early 1980s gave way to steadily lower nominal interest rates, irrespective of the fluctuations of real rates. For each country, therefore, the affordability of its household debt level requires specific scrutiny.

When it comes to non-financial business debt, the limits of affordability are clearer over the long run, though such debt can be highly cyclical. In general, this review focuses chiefly on *net* non-financial business debt. This raises dangers, as one company's strong cash position is not available to another with debts and no cash. And in any case, the cash position cannot be run down to zero. But we are concerned with a general, nationwide assessment of the sustainability of debt. There will always be individual companies going bust. The question is, what are the desirable limits for the aggregates? As we have been through a decade in which the cash position of companies in most developed countries has improved significantly relative to measures such as gross operating cash flow (pre-depreciation, ie, EBITDA) or pre-interest profit (EBIT), it would give rise to an unduly alarmist conclusion to ignore the cash that in many cases mitigates net debt. Nonetheless, it is desirable to keep a weather eye on gross debt.

Should the denominator of the debt ratio be EBITDA or EBIT, the difference being depreciation? The normal corporate-finance answer is EBITDA. But this reflects the source of the question, which tends to be how much debt a leveraged buy-out (LBO) can bear. The normal M&A rule of thumb is that debt at five times EBITDA becomes 'junk' – or 'high leverage' if one is being polite. However, in a typical LBO, the firm being bought has unexploited potential – often inefficient management of assets, or strippable assets, either non-core or more valuable as stand-alone assets than subsumed in the larger entity. The intention is often to starve the target of fresh investment, or at least cut it back, while maximising the yield of existing assets. Once the firm is turned round, it can be managed for the longer term, probably involving a higher rate of capital spending than in the turn-round.

For an economy, though, or rather its non-financial business sector, the flow of cash represented by depreciation should not typically be regarded as available for debt service, either interest or principle. This suggests that EBIT rather than EBITDA is the flow of income sustainably available over time to service debt. Equally, on the liberal side of the analysis, the non-financial business debt level in an economy should not require to be repaid – provided debt is not so high that a large tranche of firms is likely to be knocked out by normal downward shifts in the business cycle. So provided balance sheets have sufficient equity, and EBIT covers interest due by a sufficient margin, there is no reason for 'debt service' by the non-financial business sector in aggregate to include repayment – even though that might often be necessary for an individual firm financing a project, just as it would be for a household taking out a mortgage.

In Figure 21 (p. 149 above) both EBITDA and EBIT are shown as the denominator for non-financial business debt, to judge its sustainability. Aside from the fact that the whole economy's business sector can, if absolutely necessary, cut back investment to improve net cash flow, this dual approach is mandated by the very different depreciation flows in different countries. Thus, US business sector depreciation is 12% of GDP, versus 21% for Japan. The higher Japanese number represents a blend of low capital productivity, wasteful investment over decades, and a correspondingly long period of low growth, slowing the denominator of this ratio. It follows that the depreciation charge in Japan grossly overstates that economy's future replacement-investment needs, and contains cash flow that could quite safely be devoted to debt service. Use of EBIT only for the non-financial debt ratio in Japan would lead to understatement of debt capacity.

Contrariwise, Japan's slow growth counts against business debt capacity. If we consider the economic value of the capital of a firm with an indefinite, constant growth rate, it is defined (in discounted cash flow terms) by a formula whose denominator is (r–g), where 'r' is the rate of discount (blend of the cost of equity and of debt) and 'g' the growth rate. Japan's growth discontinuity in 1990 presented an interesting break-point in its business debt capacity. Its growth rate went in a step-shift downward from about 5% in the 1980s to 1% in the 1990s. If we take the cost of capital ('r', the discount rate) to be 7%, then (r–g), the denominator, shifts from 2% (7% minus 5%) to 6% (7% minus 1%). This increase of 3-times in the denominator effectively cuts the value of the firm by two thirds. If we think of debt capacity as a certain maximum proportion of the value of the firm, then it too is cut by two thirds in the Japanese circumstances of the early 1990s.

It follows that it was the collapse of growth (owing to gross supply-side weakness) that left Japanese businesses seriously over-leveraged. As this was understood only slowly by the ruling elite, reactions were slow, so the process of business deleverage only started when cash flow was severely squeezed by the clampdown of spring 1997, itself necessitated by the overheating that arose from unawareness of how much potential growth had been damaged compared to expectations based on the pre-1990 experience. Much the same is true of China today, so the question of whether China has a debt problem is closely bound up with one's view of future Chinese growth potential, making it a subject by itself, rather than part of a general study covering mostly mature economies with only moderate growth trends.

The last sector to consider is the financial sector. In the run-up to the 2007–08 financial crisis, analysts tended to ignore financial sector debt as being a 'pass-through'. The sector's assets largely comprise debts of non-financial sectors, households, non-financial businesses or governments. This means that adding the financial sector's debts to a nation's total would result in double-counting. But the crisis invalidated the idea that one could ignore the financial sector's debts, even if it remains broadly correct in normal circumstances. The problem was that the pre-crisis financial sector was neither effectively subject to official regulation nor prudent in self-regulation. Though adequate regulations existed in most countries, they were generally not properly enforced. As a result, the financial sector's 'assets', against which its debts were the 'pass-through' – were not worth what the balance sheet said. This is little surprise given the volume of banks making (for example) 'Ninja' mortgage loans ('no income, no job, or assets' – or even application form in many cases).

In general, with a properly regulated banking sector, the financial sector's debts should be irrelevant to the nation's debt capacity. But the recent crisis has shown that severe write-downs can sometimes be required that involve the government's support, throwing all or much of the financial sector's debt into the government gross, if not its net, debt. In the US, for example, the contingent call of Freddie Mac and Fannie Mae on the federal government's support, means that half of the financial debt ratio, itself some 100% of GDP, is supported by the US national credit. Clearly, the actual potential net liability of the federal government arising from problems at 'Fannie and Freddie' is far less than this. But it may be prudent to add notionally a portion of the financial sector's debt above a certain ratio to adjust the concept of government debt. This too has to be considered country by country, with the most extravagant risks associated with Ireland, and, less so and in different ways, the UK and Switzerland as well as the US. But in this book potential problems are dealt with by looking at where excessive non-financial leverage – mostly private-sector – is likely to threaten the future value of banks' assets (which are chiefly the non-financial sector's debts).

## Household debt

Since US household debt excesses were the primary cause of the 2007–09 financial crisis, establishing the feasible sustainable level for it helps to set the criteria for looking at other countries. But their experience is likely to be less malignant unless their household debt levels are much higher than America's. The US has a higher ratio of personal disposable income to GDP than any other country being considered here so all the countries except Spain (in Table 2, p. 144 above) with household debt vulnerability have, or had at the peak of the crisis, higher ratios of debt to disposable income than the US. The US ratio peaked at just under 130% of net disposable income at the end of 2007. At that stage the 'financial obligations ratio' (FOR) of home-owning households was 17.6%, against a 1980s–1990s average of 15%. The FOR is a broad measure of debt service relative to disposable income, and in this case includes the income of home-owners without mortgages. This means the debt-service burden of those with mortgages is much higher than those percentages imply.

The logic of the crisis-provoking 17.6% FOR versus the 14–16% range prevailing up to 2002 is that an FOR one sixth above the sustainable mean (ie, 17.6% vs. 15%) was enough to provoke crisis. As the debt ratio was just under 130% at the time, the implied long-run sustainable level of debt – at the interest rates typical in the middle of the last decade – was about 110% of disposable income (ie, six sevenths of the 128.6% ratio when the crisis started). The ratio had fallen by 2011 Q1 to 112.6%, helped by growth in disposable income, not least through a drop in the average impact of tax and social security payments from 20.5% of total personal income to 17.2%. (The actual debt was down by 4%, accounting for only a quarter of the fall in the ratio.) With lower interest rates also helping the FOR, it had dropped to 14.8%, in the middle of the sustainable range – and in countries such as Britain and Spain with a preponderance of floating-rate mortgages lower interest rates would have had an even greater effect. Nonetheless, the level of US household debt cannot be considered sustainable until it yields a 15% FOR with normal interest rates, ie, assuming c.2½% growth and 2% inflation, some 4% for Fed funds, 5% for US Treasuries, 6% for mortgages. So the 110% number for the US remains 'par'.

With this background, it is remarkable that UK household debt problems seem to have been confined to the badly mismanaged Northern Rock fiasco. In 2009, for instance, the UK debt ratio to *net* disposable income was 161% (on Eurostat data) versus the US 125%. (This net income number for the UK is only available annually, well in arrears.) Four factors that might account for the US having a crisis that the UK scarcely suffered are the degree of house-price fall, the ease with which Americans can 'walk away' from mortgage obligations, the extent of floating-rate mortgages with their ability to be relieved by low interest rate policies, and simple differences in national habits, in this case willingness to curtail other consumption of goods and services to be able to own a home.

On the house price front, US house prices had been falling significantly for more than a year by mid-2007, when the looming subprime crisis became apparent. British prices were still going up until autumn, 2007. Since mid to late 2007 US prices are down another 30% or so, while British prices fell by 17% in a year and a half from autumn, 2007, but then rallied 9%, before renewed slippage of 3% over the past year. This testifies to the continuing seriousness of the US housing crisis, and structural overhang of excess housing, a problem that Britain avoided owing to the difficulty of getting planning permission to build new houses. But it does not go far to explain why Britain has not had a significant mortgage default crisis at any stage over the past 3–4 crisis years.

Different national laws and habits, and the preponderance of floating-rate mortgages in Britain, seem to be the chief cause of different debt tolerances. In the US, mortgages in most states are secured on the house, but are not an unsecured obligation of the borrower. This astonishing laxity of US banking practice makes it simple for an over-burdened borrower to escape repayment obligations by simply abandoning the house. In normal conditions, this would not happen much, but the shattering crash of US house prices, totalling one third, has ensured negative equity in an estimated 30% of all mortgaged homes, despite huge repossessions, for a total of $750 billion of negative equity – versus total home mortgage debt outstanding of $10 trillion. Nor surprisingly, many US home-owners have chosen to default. The level of aggregate debt is significantly lower at which such decisions become rational on a national scale, provoking crisis.

When it comes to pure national habit, the US and UK household debt ratios both soared in the ten years to 2007, but the British one by significantly more. So the fact that defaults have not been a big issue in Britain points to the current debt ratio, though very high, as bearable. US debt to net disposable income went up from 87% to 129% between 1997 and 2007; Britain's household debt to gross disposable income from 103% to 173% over the same period. (Britain's gross disposable income is typically 5% larger than the net measure.) The American increase, measured as 'percent of percent', was 48%, versus Britain's 68%.

The broader effects of national habit cannot be isolated from one particular national habit, however, that of using floating-rate mortgages in Britain. The result of this was that interest payments by UK households fell from a peak of 11.1% of disposable income in 2008 Q1 to 7.0% in 2010 Q4, the bulk of the fall being in the year after 2008 Q3. Self-evidently, this payment relief hugely improved the ability of people to sustain their mortgages without default. Combined with longer-term willingness to accept consumption of a lesser proportion of disposable income, lack of ability to walk away from loans and tighter housing supply – holding up prices better in the recent unfavourable conditions

– this has meant a remarkably high debt ratio has not caused the same problems in Britain as in the US, whose households brought down the global financial 'house of cards'.

Nonetheless, it is doubtful whether current debts are regarded as acceptable in the longer term, so the deleverage effects should be felt through the economy for some years – not least because British interest rates are likely to go up, raising substantially the burden of the existing debt level. This is in contrast with the US, where the crisis has brought the debt ratio down further and faster, but at the expense of shattering the housing industry and, via house prices, overall household wealth. Under any scenario, this must restrain British growth. Any growth will depend on a cheaper real exchange rate stimulating demand, to offset these household financial constraints. But such devaluation is likely to mean greater inflation, from a level that is already a concern, implying higher interest rates and therefore worsening the household debt-service burden.

# Index